Changing the World

Creative Christian ideas
for youth groups

Ken Moser

**CHANGING
THE WORLD**
PRESS

A book by Changing the World Press

First Published December 2002
Copyright © Ken Moser 2002

Published in the UK by
The Good Book Company
Elm House, 37 Elm Road
New Malden, Surrey KT3 3HB
Tel: 0845 225 0880; Fax: 0845 225 0990
email: admin@thegoodbook.co.uk
website: www.thegoodbook.co.uk

Changing the World Press
95 Hyatts Road, Oakhurst, NSW Australia 2761

National Library of Australia
ISBN 0 958139 31 8

Cover and page design: Anthony Wallace
Typesetting: Greg Mills

Printed in China

Preface

Greetings. This book is designed to be a resource to help you run weekly youth gatherings that are Christian, promote good relationships, and are enjoyable at the same time.

The book will focus on the weekly youth gathering (some call it the meeting or fellowship). We will give you some helpful tips, hints and programme segments designed to be solid in content and helpful to the group. These ideas are to be read in partnership with the book, *Changing the World through Effective Youth Ministry*, which discusses the general strategy of running an effective youth ministry. In it I outline a strategy I call 'Build, Reach and Flow'. I will refer to this book quite often. If you haven't read it you may want to find a copy.

We are very keen to help groups change the world by running meetings that aim to glorify God, build strong disciples of Jesus, promote group unity, reach out to their friends, and do so while having a great time together.

If you'd like to make contact or if you have any ideas you'd like to share for the next volume please contact me at kjmoser@hotmail.com. You can also check out our website: effectiveyouthministry.com.

Read on!

Ken and Julie Moser

Acknowledgments

A big thank you to Julie Moser and Sarah Leisk for their much needed help in the composition of this book.

To the many people who helped form the ideas in the following pages. Where possible, I have tried to give due credit. Thanks also to Poolie for his helpful comments.

To Gary and Carol O'Brien, thanks for being deeply committed friends.

Finally, thanks to the team from Stuntmasters and the International Rebiblification Association. You have inspired countless generations of young people across the world to take the Bible seriously and to bring their Bibles to youth groups.

This book is dedicated to all those youth leaders and groups trying to build with gold, silver and costly stones. Press on brothers! Press on sisters!

Thanks to the God of second chances. May this be to His glory...

Contents

Long ago in a suburb far away

Once upon a time there was a young man training at a Bible college. He loved Jesus and was eager to change the world for him.

After a year at college, one of the lecturers told him that he must get a part-time job working for a church, 'This is part of your education and will help sharpen your ministry skills,' he said. He quickly found a church that was desperate for a youth leader and which had some cash. 'Perfect,' he thought.

Now this young man didn't really have much idea of how to run a Christian youth group. However, he knew what he wanted to achieve. He was eager to see a thriving group made up of young men and women wanting to follow Jesus. He wanted a group that would love each other and would reach out to those who weren't Christians. He wanted a group that would have some impact on the local community. So he found some 'experts' and asked their advice. He spent time with several people who had gone before him and were experienced in running Christian youth groups. They were very helpful. They told him to run a group on a Friday night with an hour or so of games and activities and then try to have a Bible study, prayer and small groups. 'That sounds great!' he said. The experts also told him to go to the local Christian bookstore. 'There'll be plenty of helpful books on how to run a youth programme,' they said. They were right. He found dozens of books on games and activities designed to produce an evening of way out, crazy, full on, wild fun.

He took over the reins of the youth group and it was a raging success. He could tell a funny story, he was a natural at running games that were exciting and he even had an American accent, which delighted the kids. He also learned how to run a tight programme. He had an hour of fun and games, a short talk and then discussion groups followed by supper and another game. For two years the group grew and grew. He started with eight kids and when he left, there were nearly 30 young people who were devoted to the Friday night fellowship.

At the end of two years, it was time to move on. He took a job in another part of town to gain some different ministry experience. He felt sad, yet he knew that the programme would continue. 'The kids will be okay,' he assured himself.

Soon after he left however, there were problems. The new leader didn't have an American accent and the games weren't as much fun. Many left. The group numbers dropped from 30 to half a dozen or so.

He always felt sad when he thought about the group. 'Why didn't they stay with the Christian faith,' he would ask himself, 'when they had such a good time each Friday night?'

That's not the end of the story. Fifteen years later the members held a reunion. Many of the young people, who now were not so young, came along. Even the old leader showed up. It was a fun time. Yet, the old leader was deeply troubled. Most of the people now showed no desire to follow Jesus. They couldn't be bothered. While it was great to see all the old gang again, his heart was heavy for many weeks.

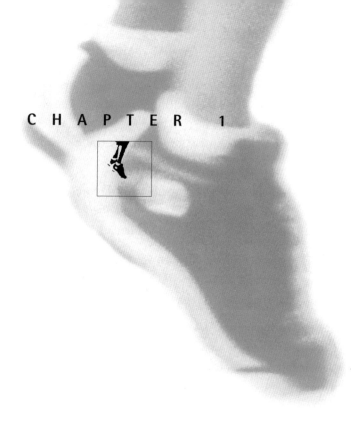

CHAPTER 1

First things first!

Don't you feel sorry for the poor guy in the previous story? He had devoted two years of his life to building up a youth group yet he saw little or no fruit. While there was a great boost in numbers, he saw very few kids turn to Christ and follow him long term. Ultimately, there was nowhere near the impact for the Kingdom of God that he had hoped.

Yet, take heart, he learned his lesson and won't make the same mistake again! The lesson for us all is that what we do in our weekly youth meetings is of the utmost importance. We must be clear about what we are trying to achieve and how we are going to do it.

I am going to assume that your aim in youth ministry is to produce disciples of Christ; disciples who will last the distance. These young men and women will be the backbone of a youth ministry that will be truly effective in changing this world for Jesus. I am also going to assume that you intend to run weekly youth group meetings that will achieve that goal.

The formula is simple – concentrate primarily on running a group that is committed to being Christian. As the group prays and reads the Bible together it will encourage the members to live lives that reflect Jesus to the outside world.

The goal is to produce strong Christian young people who will reach out to their friends, neighbours, family and workmates. They will do this naturally as they live godly lives. In addition, run targeted evangelistic events designed to clearly present Christ to the outsider.

Make sure that the groups 'flow', that is, endeavour to keep the young people you have built up and reached by running groups that are age appropriate. As the kids grow up, move them into a group designed for that stage of their lives. The obvious example of this is having a junior youth group ready to take the kids who are moving up from Sunday school. You need to plug the gaps that can cause you to lose kids.

I call this way of thinking 'Build, Reach and Flow' (see *Changing the World*, chapter 5, p32.)

This book is designed to go a bit deeper than *Changing the World* when it comes to the actual 'how to' of running a weekly youth gathering. Hopefully, you will find ideas that will be Christian, helpful for building good relationships within the group, and are a lot of fun. We can't promise miracles (that is up to God) nor will we make empty promises based on programming tricks or gimmickry. All the ideas have been tried and tested by groups in different contexts in many parts of the world.

Traps for youth leaders

If you wish to set up and run a weekly youth programme that will produce real long-term results, there are a number of traps to avoid. Let's examine a few common mistakes youth leaders often make.

Big Mistake #1: The False Spectrum

Many of us see youth ministry as a wide spectrum. At one end is the 'Rage'. The Rage is a programme of entertainment and attraction. It contains a high proportion of games, and activities designed to be fun with little or no meaningful content. A typical evening might be an hour or so of games and activities, a short talk (maybe some discussion groups) and then another game or two. The aim is to have a variety of activities and entertainment, with a small amount of Christian input. This style of programme is very common, very tiring and in most cases, has a low success rate.

At the other end of the spectrum is 'Full-on Bible Study & Discipleship'. The leaders see youth group as a place of serious commitment to Christ. The evening (or afternoon) meetings are built around solid Bible study and prayer. They hope to cut through the obvious shallowness of the Rage and produce real followers of Jesus. However, they find that the whole thing is a bit heavy. The group doesn't attract as many nonChristians as the Rage and soon becomes quite dreary. Sure, some kids are being well discipled, but there must be a way of producing disciples without putting them to sleep! (See the ballad of Bruce and Neil in *Changing the World through effective youth ministry*.)

The majority of us run a programme somewhere in the middle of the spectrum. (I call this 'the cocktail' or the 'half-half'). This is where we try to run a programme containing the good elements of the activities-based Rage programme. We hope the group will be fun and exciting with new people coming every week. Yet, we also want a group with the real devotion to Christ that is found in the full-on Bible study programme. Therefore, we run 45 minutes to an hour of games and fast paced activities, then have a short Bible talk, discussion groups, a bite to eat and everyone goes home.

There is a common flaw in each of these models. We try to make our programmes fun and often the fun is not Christian. We then have a Christian segment, which isn't fun. We believe it is an either/or situation. The programme can be entertaining and attractive (the fun), or there is the Christian time (the truth). There is a false dichotomy or split in our programmes between having fun and doing the Christian things we feel we must do. We need to throw this whole idea of youth ministry out of the window. Get rid of any idea that a Christian youth gathering cannot be both Christian and fun. We must have fun doing Christian things (like meeting together, encouraging each other, prayer, and studying the Bible).

Big Mistake #2: Building with straw (Choko programming)

In Australia we have a plant called the choko. Choko's are great. While the fruit has no flavour of its own, they are used to fill up whatever is missing in certain food dishes. For instance, if you are making pie and you don't have enough apples, grab a choko and throw it in. It takes on the flavour of the apples already there, and fills out the pie.

While the choko is a great food additive, it is not as good as the real fruit. It is only an additive. You never make a 'choko pie'. When it comes to youth ministry, we must be careful that we don't fill our programmes with choko! The temptation for many youth leaders is to fill the programme with contents that serve no real purpose. Some things that we do can actually work against us rather than for us.

In the book of 1 Corinthians the apostle Paul warns us that we must be careful how we build in our ministry. I'll remind you of his words.

> By the grace God has given me, I laid a foundation as an expert builder, and someone else is building on it. But each one should be careful how he builds. For no one can lay any foundation other than the one already laid, which is Jesus Christ. If any man builds on this foundation using gold, silver, costly stones, wood, hay or straw, his work will be shown for what it is, because the Day will bring it to light. It will be revealed with fire, and the fire will test the quality of each man's work. If what he has built survives, he will receive his reward. If it is burned up, he will suffer loss; he himself will be saved, but only as one escaping through the flames. (1 Corinthians 3:10–15)

The message is clear, build with good materials (gold, silver and costly stones). Avoid building with anything that will not stand on the Day of Judgment. With this in view, we must be careful that we don't fill our programmes with straw! Our weekly meetings or fellowship nights must not contain items that only fill in time, or burn up some energy.

If this is the case, either change your programme or shorten the length of your meeting. Certain games or high energy activities often fall into this trap. We justify them by claiming that they promote getting to know each other, good mixing or team building. In reality, they are usually nothing more than straw. They serve no purpose other than filling in time. Many of us shrug our shoulders and say, 'How else are we going to provide young people with a good time and fill up two hours at the same time?'

Quite often we don't know how to run 'Christian' programming that is truly fun and attractive. We sweat through giving a short talk from the Bible, sometimes bribing the kids along the way, 'If you sit still and listen for five minutes then we'll play another game'. We try to have a group prayer time but often end up taking silly requests and when it's time to pray all we hear is an eerie silence or the occasional cough. Many of us would never dare to sing or have a time of praise and worship. You'd be better off trying to control a herd of wildebeests barehanded. Some leaders find that their groups pray and study the Bible because it is important, but it certainly isn't the highlight of the evening. We must learn how to correct this.

Big Mistake # 3: No committed core or community

Some of us have run groups built on a shifting base of sand. This sand is our desperate hope for commitment from the members of our youth group. Our great desire is for the young people in the youth group to become committed to Christ and to the group as a community. We hope that our group will grow as new people come, hear about Christ and stay. A few groups are doing this quite successfully. The majority are on a constant treadmill of disappointment as their numbers are constantly shifting. Furthermore, we rarely attract as many nonChristians as we would like. Those we do attract are often rowdy and come to the group with mixed motives (a great social night and to meet the opposite sex). We need to learn how to develop groups that are driven by a committed core of Christian young people whose top priority is following Christ.

Furthermore, much of our programming actually hinders rather than fosters the development of good relationships. Think about your group. Do the kids ring each other up during the week to say hello? Do they ring some one who has not showed up for a few weeks? How about the humour in the group? Do they laugh with each other or at each other? When new people come, does the warmth of the relationships between group members immediately strike them? Or, is there a large amount of complaining within the group? Are there cliques that exclude other members of the youth group (or newcomers)? The Bible couldn't be clearer about the fact that our groups need to be places of kindness, selflessness and love. Quite often the fact that our programmes are designed to entertain promotes something contrary to what should be there. We aim for love and joy but we programme mindless activities and entertainment. We need to focus on producing a group that reflects Christian love, where good relationships are fostered and developed week by week.

Fixing the problem!

Some of the above problems are deep and it would be silly to suggest that there are easy solutions. However, there are ways of making our programmes more effective. We need to develop weekly youth gatherings that promote three things:

1. Good solid Christian content.

2. Loving Christian relationships within the group.

3. Enjoyment in being Christian!

It is important to realise that we are not giving you a magic formula that will automatically transform your group. The ideas in the following pages will work only if the leaders are willing to serve the kids and be committed to running a group that is thoroughly Christian and enjoyable at the same time. Be prepared to persevere for several weeks or even months to see these new ideas for your weekly gathering take root and produce fruit. It took many months of hard work in my own youth group before we saw any fruit at all.

How this book will work

We will give you some practical tools to help you develop a youth gathering/meeting that is Christian, group building and enjoyable. We will try to provide segments and programming content that will assist you to be effective in building the Kingdom of God in your area.

We will discuss how to put it all together to form an easy to run, well structured time for your group.

We will focus on how to bring these elements into your weekly meeting and introduce change into your program.

Please note that the items in the following chapters occur in the order that they can appear in your weekly program (ie a Spotlight followed by a Bible game etc.)

There is a resource section in the back with questions, memory verses and other goodies to help you along.

Read on!

CHAPTER 2

The art of the great start

Key thought:	It is crucial that every youth group meeting/gathering begins well.
Reflection:	Spend time reflecting on the weekly meeting/fellowship night. What are you hoping to accomplish? How can the first few minutes together help you to achieve this? Are you 'starting well' or is the start working against the goals you have set for the meeting?

Why a 'Great Start'?

A great start sets the tone for the rest of the time together. The whole meeting suffers if you start in a dull, boring way or if are you are disorganised. A good start will send a message that the next hour or two is going to be worthwhile. For the newcomer, the start of the night can make an impression. For Christians (or regular members), the start reminds them that the weekly youth group is meeting because of Jesus. You want those who know Jesus to get to know him better. You are hoping that those who don't know him will come to know him. You want the group to become a close, loving community; not just a group of individuals seeking entertainment but a living, loving body of believers. This is the body of Christ seeking to change the world. Everything that you do must reflect this fact and help promote it.

Golden Rule #1 Begin with a welcome

Make sure you gather all the young people together and give a clear welcome to start the meeting. Follow this with a prayer asking for God's blessing on your time together. It's amazing how many groups start with nothing more than, 'Hey come on everybody, form two rows and let's play a game to begin'. This is a disaster.

Three reasons why no welcome spells trouble:

1. No welcome says there is no group identity. One of your goals must be to take a group of individuals and turn them into a Christian community. That is, a body of friends and people who relate well to each other and reflect Jesus to each other. To begin your time together with nothing more than a quick hello and the beginning of a game sends a message that this is nothing more than a collection of individuals. A clear, organised welcome from a leader can help to show people that they are a group.

2. No welcome indicates there is no leadership. A good meeting has good leadership. Some of us are struggling with a group of young people who may be rowdy or difficult to handle. One way to win them over is to show them that you are there to lead them into a better way. A clear start from the leadership will help set the tone of the meeting.

3. A youth gathering that begins with nothing more than playing a game can lead to unproductive rowdiness.[1] The kids are so hyped up by the opening games/activities that they never settle down for the more beneficial part of the evening. You will find that they have a hard time listening to the talk or participating in the discussion groups. You may also find that some kids will turn up late because they can't be bothered showing up on time.

A clear welcome will start the meeting on the right foot. The welcome must show everyone that the group is gathered together because of Jesus (an opening prayer is a must, more on this in a minute).

How to Welcome

A good welcome is fairly straightforward. It can be fun or serious. You can begin on a humorous note (a joke or funny story) or talk about why the group is meeting ('because we are a group of Christians, to get to know Jesus better'). You can simply state why you hold the meeting, what the group is going to do for the next hour or so and ask for God's blessing.

---

1. Some rowdiness can be positive as it shows the kids are comfortable enough to be themselves and are excited to be meeting. A rowdy atmosphere can be good or it may be an indication of disorderly, disrespectful behaviour.

Three simple guidelines:

Be yourself

Don't try to be someone you're not. If you are not naturally a comedian, don't force it. If you find it hard to stand in front of a group of people and speak, keep it brief and to the point. Not wanting to be in the spotlight is not a crime.

Be clear

Work through what you are going to say and say it simply and clearly. If you need to write down some notes, do so.

Be brief

Keep it short and to the point. You are trying to get the meeting off to a good start, not to entertain them for twenty minutes. If you are inexperienced at this, be careful, when you are in front of a crowd time has a way of standing still. You may think you are talking for 30 seconds or so and later you find that your welcome went for over five minutes!

P.S.

It helps if you smile. It is much easier to listen to someone who smiles than to someone who looks like they are telling you to clean your room!

Suggested 'welcomes':

Simple and straightforward

'Welcome to youth group (or whatever you call it). Tonight is going to be a great night as we ... (fellowship, pray, have discussion groups, eat ...). I'll pray and ask the Lord to give us a great night!'

You tell me and I'll tell you

You could ask them this question, 'What are we going to do tonight?' The group will no doubt give you some responses. You could then tell them what the programme consists of and then say, 'Let's ask God to help us!'

A joke, funny story, or humorous observation

You could open with a funny story; something that you have read or heard about or something that has happened to you; something relating to the programme that you read in the papers or found on the internet. This is an effective way to begin but it can also be the most difficult. If it falls flat, the evening may take some time to recover.

Serious story, current events

A story that is in the news can be a powerful way to start the night. Or, you could begin by talking about something you learned about God in the previous week.

Introduce a theme for the meeting

You could begin by introducing a main theme that you have set for the night. You could simply say, 'Tonight we are going to look at ... I'll pray for us!' Or, you could begin with a personal story or illustration, a current event, a skit, a clip from a song or an appropriate activity – something to link the beginning to the topic of the message later on.

An encouraging or challenging Bible verse
It is helpful to use Hebrews 10:24,25 regularly to remind the group that you are meeting to 'spur one another on to love and good deeds and to encourage each other as the day (of judgment) approaches'.

Remember, if all else fails, or you feel ill equipped, you don't have to say anything more than, 'Welcome to youth group. I'm going to start us off by praying for our time together.'

Example

At our youth group one night the leader who was running the meeting told us a story that happened to him earlier in the week. He was waiting for his mother to pick him up from the train station. When he saw what he thought was his mother's car, he hopped in. The poor woman who was in the car screamed at him, 'Take the car, but please, please don't hurt me!' He quickly hopped out trying to explain that it was a case of mistaken identity. He went on to say what we were going to do in the youth group in case anyone was in the wrong place!

There are many, many different ways to give a welcome. I have suggested a few. Be creative, be yourself and come up with ideas that suit your group.

Golden Rule #2 Open with prayer

Many groups never open their time together with a prayer. They run a programme designed to help young people get to know God better, yet they don't ask for his help! Do not make this mistake. Make sure someone asks for God's blessing on the meeting. You do this for two reasons:

1. We need God's help if we are to do his work! Your time together is all about Jesus and his kingdom. Ask him to help.

2. Praying for the night lets everyone know that we will focus on God over the next couple of hours. The Christian regular, the friend who has been brought to the group for the first time, the fringe person who comes every now and then – all these people need to be reminded (or told) that this is a place where God is honoured and is at work. A prayer at the beginning goes a long way toward showing this. Always ask for God's help to do so.

Who should pray?

Either the person leading from the front, another leader or a young person in the group should open with prayer. Sometimes I ask for a volunteer who will pray for us as we begin. Other times I invite someone to pray to start the meeting (after I have given a good welcome) and I will simply close my eyes in faith that someone will take up the offer. I am not often disappointed. (If no one prays, I'll do it myself.) Every now and then I will begin the night by asking a few members of the group to lead us in prayer. We might even have a short time of open prayer, and anyone who wants to may ask Jesus to bless our time together. This makes for a great start.[2]

HOT TIP Begin with a good question!

After a welcome and prayer, a good way to continue might be with a question that facilitates people getting to know each other. A good question can help build relationships within the group as well as bring a smile or laugh. Instead of beginning with a game built around competition or individuality, questions can help promote unity as you listen to each other's answers. Ask the whole group a question and ask them to give their answer to the person sitting next to them.

Some good questions:

Describe your week comparing it to a dessert. (You could help by giving examples such as, a good week = chocolate cheesecake; a bad week can be apple crumble or a mixture = fruit salad).

Describe your mood using a weather term (cloudy, stormy, sunny and hot etc.)

Ask them to come up with the 'perfect magazine'.

If you formed a rock band, what would call it and why?

What's the best 'wipeout' you've ever had?

Describe your week using a sporting word (a hat trick, home run, hole in one etc.)

More suggested questions are given at the back of the book on pages 115–117.

We have found that group members are more likely to talk if they are comfortable with each other. After they have spoken with the person next to them, we ask them to share their answers with the whole group. We have found that quite often it is less threatening for those who are self-conscious to answer on behalf of the person next to them than to speak for themselves.

HOT TIP Begin with a skit or dramatic answer to the question.

You can begin the meeting with a question where some of the kids come to the front of the group and act out their answers by way of skits or mime. This may be difficult at first,

---

2. You would be correct in thinking that I am confident there are people in the group who are willing and able to pray this way. We wouldn't have dared to try this when the group first started. Things are different now (thank the Lord!).

but in time, with some prompting and help from the leaders, you may find this to be a great way to begin.

Examples

Talk about one thing they did during the week/weekend that was special, fun or unusual and then mime it for the group to guess. (Or, say what you are looking forward to this week/weekend).

On Father's/Mother's day ask them to say what is unique about their dad/mother and act it out in front of the group. (Be sensitive towards those young people who come from difficult home situations.)

At the beginning of a new season, ask people to act out what they like best about that season.

On the first day of Winter we asked for volunteers to perform the 'best shiver', which was a hoot.

At the first meeting back after school holidays, invite them to act out what they spent most of their time doing.

HOT TIP When you set the question for the young people in your group, don't tell them that you are going to ask for volunteers to come to the front and act it out. Otherwise some members of the group will give a false answer (answers designed to be easy to act out). Ask the question, let the group discuss it for a minute or so and then tell them that you would like a couple of volunteers to act out the other person's answer.

HOT TIP Link the question to the talk

Link the question/dramatic answer to the Bible study. If you were studying the creation story of Genesis you could ask them to act out their favourite animal. If you were looking at the book of Jonah they could mime a fish or ocean creature for everyone to guess. On one occasion, we were running our youth meeting based around the theme 'love your enemies'. After a welcome and opening prayer, we asked the young people to 'create the perfect enemy'. They discussed it among themselves (with the person next to them) and then we asked for a few volunteers to come up and draw the perfect enemy on the whiteboard. All sorts of hideous creations were drawn! This was a good launching point for the rest of the night.

Icebreakers or mixer games

If you are a typical youth leader, you will have purchased at least one book on games and youth group activities. Almost all of them contain a section on mixer games or icebreakers designed to help the group mix, mingle and reduce any fears there may be when a group of individuals are together in the same room. Mixers can be a helpful addition to your meeting.

Some words of warning:

Mixers presuppose that the group needs help getting to know each other. This can be the case if your group is just starting out. However, it is important that you focus on activities that produce real relationships; such as good small groups and camps.[3] Promote events where you spend a healthy dose of quality time together. Your aim must be to build into your overall programme elements that truly develop good relationships. A mixer can be good, but generally it is a shallow way of bringing about real relationship.

Mixers can be just another excuse to run games or other activities designed to produce excitement and good times. Games are not the best way to promote fun and good relationships. True fun comes out of loving relationships in a safe, comfortable setting. Mixers can be a part of this, but quite often you can get by without them.

Mixers can make it difficult to move on to the next item in your program if you are having problems with crowd control or over-excited members in your group. If it's difficult getting the group to settle down, it would be better not to get them excited in the first place.

Despite the negative points, there are some good mixers that can be used from time to time.

Make sure your mixers mix!
Many of them don't. They just force people to move around making brief contact with each other. Critically examine the mixer to make sure that it will really help people in your group get to know each other better.

Example
You may know the game 'People Bingo'. This is where you have a sheet of paper made up of a grid with many squares. Each square has a statement like, 'find someone with red hair', or, 'someone who goes to a different school'. The goal is to run around and find someone who can sign the relevant square. The winner is the first person to fill out every square on the sheet. This game does not promote mixing! It is nothing more than running around making brief contact. Here's a way of turning this non-mixer into a more effective group builder: if you are able, make the individual squares much bigger. Instead of having the group gather signatures, have them draw a sketch of the appropriate person. For instance, in a square that says, 'find a person who has red hair', find and draw that person. You can also add a few questions designed to gather information in each square.

Run mixers/icebreakers that promote good conversation
For instance, run a 'find your match' mixer. This is where someone stands up (or climbs on a chair) and shouts out, 'Find someone who goes to a different school than you'. The group then rushes around forming pairs of young people who go to different schools. At this point the leader can ask a question that will facilitate discussion between two people who

---

3.   Weekly Bible study groups that meet in someone's home are the best way of building sold relationships within a big group. If you can't do this, run weekly discussion groups in your meeting. But make sure that you do not chop and change these groups too often. Keep them the same for a good length of time – at least a school term.

may never have met or don't know each other well. The leader may then ask for volunteers to tell the group about their partner's answer.

HOT TIP Providing food and music before the start facilitates natural mixing. We find it helpful to put out a bowl of chips and have some good Christian music playing before the young people arrive for the youth meeting. This provides a comfortable setting for them to 'catch up'. During this time the leaders mingle with the kids and hopefully anyone who is new is introduced around and made to feel welcome.

Mixers are a good way to meet new groups of people.
Mixers are good when there is a combined night with another youth group or if you have moved up a year group from a younger youth group. For instance, a mixer would be appropriate where you are moving up the year six kids from Sunday school.

HOT TIP A great mixer game
Sit your group in a circle and each person gives his or her full name and any reason as to why they have that name – in particular any unusual hyphenated or middle names. There may also be a reason why their parents chose those names. For most people their middle name comes from someone in the family. This game gives each person the chance to find out a little bit more about other people in the group. It can also be a lot of fun!

Final thoughts

Spend time on creative brainstorming for good ways to open the meeting. This will prevent things becoming stale. I know of one leader who keeps a pad of paper on his desk at work. When he gets an idea, he jots it down. He soon has an enormous bank of ideas to use.

Problems ... questions anyone?

What if certain kids regularly show up late?

1. Are they making a statement? In other words, are they voting with their feet? Many young people may come late because they are committed to the old way of doing things. They may want the choko and not the Christian content. You may find some young people will begin to drop off when the programme becomes more solid in content. However, some young people are the other way around. They dislike the games and only want the good stuff. They got into a pattern of coming late to miss the choko. Either way, spend some time talking with them (and listening). Find out if they are willing and able to show up on time. Seek to win them over. You may have to convince them to be patient and give the group a try.

2. Start the meeting by gathering together all the young people. Educate the regulars as to when the youth meeting starts. You could do some humorous skits on it. All of us are late at one time or another. However, continual lateness shows a serious lack of respect.

This (like most other problems) can only be solved by good relationships. The young people who are late must respect the leaders, the other kids and the programme itself.

What if the group is made up primarily of nonChristians who will freak out if we begin with prayer?

If that is the case, there are more serious issues at stake than a few cosmetic changes. Why do they come? Is it to hear about Jesus or to have a good night out at the leader's expense? If your group is made up of people who are there for no other reason than to have a fun night out, it is time to make some serious changes.[4]

What if group members don't know each other well or find it difficult to relate to each other?

You must work on developing good relationships. The solution is not to run games or activities that produce sweat and not much else. Are there small groups? If not, begin straight away (at the very least, start small groups in your weekly meeting which keep the same young people with the same leader). Are you running regular camps or days away to foster community and help the young people to truly get to know each other?

My experience has been that if you persevere with your programme many of the kids will come on board eventually. Please realise that they will only do this if they trust and respect you (and the other leaders).

---

4.   See *Changing the World*, chapter 15.

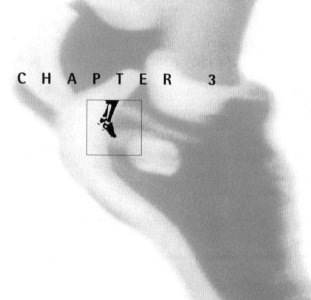

C H A P T E R   3

Spotlight

Key thought:	Get to know the group better through interviewing various individuals or subgroups.
Reflection:	How well does your group know each other? Is it a group or a collection of individuals? How can you run activities or segments in your programme that help the group to relate better to each other?

Spotlight is where the group has a chance to get to know individuals (or subgroups) in more depth. The idea is simple. The leader places someone from the group in the 'spotlight' and asks a number of questions; some are serious, and some are not so serious. The group (or someone in the group) then prays for the person 'spotlighted'.

How to run Spotlight

The person running Spotlight asks the group to stand up. He/she then slowly eliminates groups of people by making a series of statements like, 'Sit down if you are wearing red.

Sit down if you go to a private school. Sit down if you are a boy'. The person left standing is the one who is to be interviewed. The person comes to the front of the group and the leader asks some questions. They can stand on the ground or on a chair for better visibility. If you wish, you could even have a spotlight ready to shine on them!

Asking questions

The person doing the interviewing must have prepared some appropriate questions. Suggested Spotlight questions are included in the Resources on page 115. We have found it helpful to ask three types of questions:

1. General information gathering questions like: 'What is your full name? Where were you born? What is your favourite radio station?'

2. More humorous questions such as: 'If you were to run off and join the circus, what type of entertainer would you be? If you were a professional wrestler, what would your name be?'

3. Questions of a deeper (or Christian) nature: 'How long have you been a Christian? Why did you become a Christian? When you meet God, what is one thing you'll ask him?' Obviously, you do not ask questions of a Christian nature if you are not sure where the person stands with God.

Variety!

You could vary the Spotlight by beginning with everyone being seated and gradually standing up as the statements are made (instead of 'Sit down if you ...' . You say, 'Stand up if you ....'). The last person seated is the person you will meet. Or, you could have people begin with raised hands and gradually lower them. (You could do this if there are kids in your group who are in wheelchairs or find it hard to stand.)

Some guidelines

Choose the right people!

Basically, you need people who are fairly confident and can handle being in front of the group and will not be crushed or find the whole experience upsetting. The goal of Spotlight is not to hurt or embarrass people. It is to bring them before the group so that they can get to know each other better. I would add another requirement: they must be regular members of the youth group. Avoid spotlighting people who come occasionally to youth group. Spotlight can also be a good opportunity to focus on a Christian young person as a model or example.

Do not fall into the trap of choosing only the good looking or outgoing kids. Make sure you give equal opportunity to quiet kids as well. If you are unsure as to whether they will cope with it, ask them (or their small group leader) beforehand.

Choose who you will spotlight before you begin

Decide who you will Spotlight before the programme begins. This will save you a lot of headaches. Some groups have tried to decide who they are spotlighting while they are actually running Spotlight. Also, keep a record of who you Spotlight so that you don't keep doing the same people over and over!

Spotlight must be brief

Don't let Spotlight drag on and on. Keep it short and punchy.

Spotlight leaders or special guests

This can be a good chance for the group to meet new leaders or special guests (such as a guest speaker). At the end of the Spotlight, ask them to briefly tell the group how they became a Christian. Spotlight is a great way to lead into a testimony time.

Don't limit your spotlight to individuals

You can spotlight any subgroups in your group. For instance, early in the year, spotlight your leadership team. Later on, you can spotlight the small groups (such as Bible study groups), year groups, schools and so on.

Invite young people from within the group to run Spotlight

After a few weeks of leaders running Spotlight, ask a couple of young people from the group to run it. You can stand up the front with them to lend moral support. Just remember, they need to be prepared. You may also want to make sure they ask good questions, there can be a tendency to ask questions of a slightly unsavoury nature.

Don't overdo it

Run Spotlight for two or three weeks and then give it a rest for a few weeks. After the break, bring it back for another two or three weeks.

Five ways to do Spotlight

The Classic

Questions by one interviewer. The most common way to do Spotlight is with one interviewer asking questions.

The Tag team

Two interviewers, one asking serious and the other not so serious questions. When one finishes, they 'tag' the other interviewer, who then asks his or her question.

The Roving mike

An interviewer at the front with questions from the floor. One interviewer asks serious questions and another person in the crowd goes around with a 'microphone' taking questions from the floor (the other kids in the group).

The Talk Show

An interviewer with a number of 'guests'. We run this quite often in our youth group. One of the leaders sets up a desk (complete with coffee mug and microphone) and three chairs. It looks like a television talk show set. Three guests are brought in one at a time for a short interview. The host asks general questions similar to a classic spotlight. When he/she finishes with one of the guests, he/she asks them to move down a seat so that the next guest may sit down. It is a fun and relaxed way to spotlight several members of the group at once.

Up Close and Personal

A prearranged member of the group spotlights themselves (or is interviewed) with an insight into his/her life. Ask someone in the group to bring a number of items from home. These are designed to give the group a glimpse into their life so they get to know the person better. For instance, he or she could bring a favourite piece of clothing, favourite CD, or something from childhood. They could even bring a family member! If need be, you could have a leader (or competent young person) interview them to make it go more smoothly.

How to run Spotlight

Step 1:   Choose a leader or competent young person to run it.

Step 2:   Decide who you are going to spotlight.

Step 3:   Decide exactly how you are going to run it.

Step 4:   When you are running Spotlight, choose which way you will eliminate the rest of the group (i.e. gradually have them sit down).

Step 5:   Invite the spotlighted person to come to the front and be interviewed.

Step 6:   Run the interview.

Step 7:   Have someone pray for the person who has been interviewed.

C H A P T E R   4

Bible Games

Key thought:	Bible games can be a great part of your programme as a teaching tool and are a lot of fun as well.
Reflection:	How well do the young people in your group know their Bible? How can you increase their knowledge in a fun and helpful way? Is the only part of your programme geared towards learning – the study/talk/discussion groups – left to the end of the meeting? Are there ways of including teaching elements earlier in the programme?

When I was starting out in youth ministry I was a firm believer in playing lots of mindless games from the many books on the subject. One game I remember was where you had to hold an orange wedged under your chin. The goal was to pass the orange from one person to the next in a relay race. Do you know it? I was naive enough to believe that this would be a helpful exercise for group members; that as they passed a piece of fruit from one person to the next they would look into each other's eyes and see Jesus, realise that they were sinners, that Jesus died for them and rose again and that they must repent of their sins. By the time they passed the orange to the next person, they would have committed their life to the Lord! It wasn't until I watched a sixteen-year-old boy position himself next to a cute fifteen-year-old girl that I realised the last thing he was thinking about as he passed her the orange was his status with the Lord of the universe! It dawned on me that most of the games I was running were moving the group backwards rather than forwards in the Kingdom of God. Then I discovered Bible Games.

Why have a Bible Game?

We have found it helpful to replace games that have little or no purpose with games that promote Bible learning. They are based on a game or activity that is well known to the group and focus on the Bible in some way. For instance it might be built around a memory verse that the group is trying to learn. Or, it might be a game that includes questions from a previous study series. You can use a game to review something the group has learned as well as to promote the learning of new knowledge. I have found that through the efficient use of a good Bible game I can bring a group of young people with little or no knowledge of the Bible to a stage where they can have a good grasp of the basics. In any case a Bible game can be a helpful and fun part of your programme. Furthermore, they come in all shapes and sizes. Games can be rowdy or quiet. They can be calm and serious or active. However you run them, they can be used to teach the Bible in a creative and fun way.

Bible games aren't designed to produce Bible 'trivia' experts. Their aim is to give young people a grasp of basic Bible knowledge and fundamentals. They are also a great help in learning and driving home memory verses. The more young people become familiar with the Bible, the more they will tend to read it and hopefully, with the help of the Holy Spirit, put it into practice. Games can also give the group a sense of 'history'. Questions about past events like camps and socials will often make people laugh and say, 'That's right, remember when ...'.

There is an art to running a successful Bible game. Don't for a minute think that you can stand up and run a fun, effective and helpful game without preparation. It takes practice and know-how.

Golden Rules for running a good Bible game

1. Don't let the group take the game too seriously

A Bible game is meant to be fun, not a fight to the death! Try to avoid building the thing up into world war three or the ultimate battle for the salvation of mankind. While a degree of competitiveness is appropriate, your group will be going backward if things get heated. Run the game in a light-hearted, generous, and humorous way. Too many groups run games that reflect a desperate desire to 'win at all costs'. Winning is not the point; building relationships, gaining some Bible knowledge and having a good time is. Make sure your leaders lead the way in being humble and gracious, especially when it comes to losing. Many leaders reflect the 'winning is everything' mentality. The games you run must be an area where the group reflects the characteristics of the Kingdom of God.

2. Understand the game

The person running the game must know the goals of the game, the basic rules and how a team wins (or loses). This will help you to explain the game clearly and simply. It will also help when you have to make one of the inevitable judgment calls that will come your way. Kids love to argue the fine points of 'game law'. Be prepared. (You may wish to have a trial run at home or with your leadership team.) A good game is a well-understood game.

3. The rules must be crystal clear

The group needs to understand the nature of the game. My policy is that when I explain a game the first time I do not answer questions from anyone in the group. I tell the group that I will explain the rules of the game twice and then I will take questions. I have found that there are always several people in the group who will race ahead and ask questions about things you are about to explain. I explain the game (with no questions allowed), go through it again and then I take questions. Most questions have been answered by the second explanation of the rules. Don't spend too long on the rules. The point of the exercise is to have a fun game, not to haggle about the rules. It will help to keep the rules simple. Once you've played the game, you can play it in a week or two without the long introduction. Make sure there is a 'final authority'. That is, there must be someone who has the final say on the rules, how the game is played, and who can resolve disputes.

4. Be prepared – especially with good questions

I have learned the hard way that a game stands or falls with the preparation put into it. Make sure you have everything you need. Whether it is materials or people to assist you, get them ready ahead of time. If you are asking questions from the Bible, spend time beforehand thinking them through and writing them down. Think about why you are running the game and what you hope to accomplish. Therefore, ask helpful and appropriate questions.

5. Once an answer is given, that is the answer

When playing a game with questions, be firm that once an answer is given, that is the answer. There is no second chance if they realise they were wrong. Many kids will shout out an answer hoping it is correct. When they realise from your facial expression or voice that it isn't, they will shout out a new answer. This is game death. Once an answer is given, that is it. Following on from this, the game works better if it is clear that kids must raise their hand before giving an answer (if that is part of the game). Therefore, you may wish to give the group a few seconds to think about their answers before raising their hand. Once they give an answer, the leader can ask, 'Is that your final answer?' This gives them a chance to say yes or no. This is not a chance for them to change their answer, it merely lets them know that they cannot give two different answers to the same question. It will also help to clear up misunderstandings that occur.

6. Do not let the kids cheat

Fairly obvious isn't it? Take it from the king of Bible game cheaters, it is so tempting, even for Christians (and leaders!). While you mustn't take things too seriously, try to remove any cheating from a game. You may need to have some sort of penalty for those who stray from the rules (humorous penalties can often work well in this situation).

7. Ask questions designed to review or give new knowledge

Make sure that your questions are helpful. You can effectively teach many things about the Bible this way. For instance, through good games we have taught our group basic things like; the major division in the Bible (Old/New Testament), the fact that the Bible is broken up into chapters and verses, the first four books of the New Testament, who wrote various books, and so on. Much of this was completely new knowledge to our youth group kids.

We have found that it is fine to have similar questions week by week. We will often insert a new question such as, 'Who wrote the book of Romans?' The next week it becomes a review question. Soon, everyone in the group will know the answer. It then drops out of use for a few months making an occasional reappearance later on. It may be helpful for newcomers to throw in the odd sporting or current events question. And, whatever you do, do not direct questions to individuals who may be shy or get embarrassed.

Finding good questions is harder than most people think. You don't want questions that are too hard or easy. Also, be careful about taking a shortcut and buying books on 'Bible Trivia'. Most of the questions they contain are very difficult. It is much better for you to write your own questions beforehand. You will find that questions you have written will turn out to be more helpful for your group as well.

8. Some rowdiness or high energy level will be appropriate

A good game may cause the group to get excited and noisy. This can be a good sign. Do not try to suppress an appropriate level of energy. Let the group enjoy the game. Obviously, if the group goes nuts and begin to light bonfires, sacrifice small animals and burn effigies of the leader, there is a problem. Some shouting and howls of laughter are a positive indication that the game is working well. The aim is to have fun as well as convey information.

9. The game must not go on too long

Keep it a reasonable length. This will depend on the game. A memory verse game like Fill in the Blanks will take up to 20 minutes. A simple game like tic tac toe (noughts and crosses) may last only 5 minutes. Don't let games drag on. If need be, learn ways to speed up the process. You can do this by giving extra points or double rewards.

10. The game must be fun

Games are meant to be enjoyable. If you are trying a new game and it is a dud, quickly end it and move on. You might need to talk over the game with your leaders beforehand to make sure it goes well. Some games are just plain silly, others can lead to confusion and bickering. Be careful, if you run a bad game, it can make running the next one twice as difficult.

11. Turn mindless games into helpful Bible games

Before you throw away your game books, see if there are any games that you can change into something better. With a bit of effort, you can turn a mindless game into a helpful Bible game. An example of this is the numerous relay races where you throw a ball into a basket. If you don't know this game, the young people stand in teams and throw a ball into a basket. When you miss, you go to the back of your group, the next person throws and so on. Once a person gets the ball in the basket, he or she goes to the back of the group and sits down. The winner is the first team to be seated.

How about changing it to incorporate a memory verse? Keep the game exactly the same. However, each time you throw the ball you add a word from a memory verse. For instance, if the memory verse was James 1:22, 'Do not merely listen to the word, and so deceive yourselves. Do what it says.' This verse consists of fifteen words, sixteen with the reference included. Divide the group into teams of even numbers (if possible). Then break the verse into appropriate chunks. With a team of four they would have to say four words each. Each person must throw the ball into the basket and say four words of the memory verse in order. It will often take a few attempts for many of the people to throw the ball into the basket. At each try, they must say their section of the verse. Once they put the ball into the basket, they pass it to the next person in line, take a seat at the back of the group and sit down. The next person continues the memory verse. The first group to be seated wins. (This game is also in the section on Memory verses.)

Suddenly a pointless bit of straw programming becomes a helpful way to learn a great verse from the Bible. Similarly, take some time to see if there are any TV game shows that you can change into a good Bible/memory verse game. There are countless new Bible games out there waiting to be discovered. Go for it!

How to run a Bible Game

Step 1: Choose who will run this segment.

Step 2: Choose the game

Step 3: Organise everything you will need for the game.

Step 4: Explain the game to the group twice.

Step 5: Spend a brief time taking questions.

Step 6: Run the game and enjoy it.

Great Bible Games

Forming teams

When dividing people into teams, you could have boys versus girls; younger versus older (year 7-8 versus year 9); one year versus the rest (year 9 versus 'the world' or 'the barbarians'). Or, simply divide the room into two sides get them to give themselves a name and maybe even a 'war cry'.

1. Fill in the Blanks

A Bible verse is written up in blanks on an overhead or whiteboard.

— — — — —   — — — —

(Answer: 'Jesus wept'. John 11:35. I would suggest that you use a longer verse!)

Each team is asked a question, one at a time. If they answer correctly, they choose a letter of the alphabet. They can choose any letter at all (to speed things up they can choose two or three letters).

If the letter is in the verse it is written in the appropriate blanks. As the blanks slowly fill up, they will be able to attempt a guess at the verse.

Note

- A team may attempt to guess the verse only when they have answered a question correctly.
- The way I play, if a team answers incorrectly, the other team receives the same question as a 'freebie' and then has their turn (in other words, they get two turns in a row).
- To win, someone from the group must say the verse perfectly.
- Be prepared, it is tougher than you think to write the letters in the appropriate blanks. (It will help if the person filling in the letters in the verse has memorised the verse.)
- This game can take a while, so programme accordingly. (Also, kids will often choose odd letters like z, x or q. Be prepared for this, either by excluding these letters or by giving them a second chance to choose a letter.)
- This is a great game for introducing a new memory verse.
- A variation of this game is to not have blanks for each letter but for each word. You could call it 'Fill in the Words'. Under each blank is written a number.

For example:

_____	_____	_____	_____
1	2	3	4

When a team answers a question correctly they ask for a whole word to be written above the number they choose. (For instance, Romans 10:9 needs 26 spaces for 26 words)

When a team answers correctly, they choose a number which then reveals the word. So, for John 11:35, you would write up two blank lines with the numbers 1 and 2 written underneath (this would turn out to be a very short game!). When the group has answered a question correctly, and thinks they are able to say the whole verse, they are allowed to try to complete the blanks. This variation can speed up the process if necessary.

2. Quiz Show

Write a number of categories at the top of an overhead/whiteboard (for instance, Old Testament; memory verses, Youth group events/history). Attach envelopes below the categories and give each envelope a value in ascending order (OT for 20; OT for 40; OT for 60; and OT for 80). Place questions into each envelope—the higher the score, the harder the question. Each team gets to choose an envelope and answer a question. If they get it right they get the points, if they get it wrong, the other team gets to attempt an answer. The team with the highest score wins. (This game can take 20-30 minutes to run so be prepared.)

Note

- You can run your whole meeting like a Quiz Show with various elements of the programme in some of the envelopes. For instance, you might have OT for 40= the prayer time. The group receives the points and whoever is scheduled to run the prayer time stands up and leads it. The game then continues.

3. Tic Tac Toe (Noughts and crosses)

Set up nine chairs like a noughts and crosses board. Form two teams and direct questions to alternate teams. If they get it right they go and stand on a chair. The first team with three in a row wins. (You can play this using a noughts and crosses grid on an overhead/whiteboard if your group has only a few members.)

4. Scripture Pictures

Have a list of items (hopefully related to one topic, for instance, if you are studying Jonah, include words like fish, boat, and storm, but also insert words like your minister's name or youth group). Break up into teams of perhaps four people, and give each team a piece of paper and a pen. Each team sends a representative to see the leader, who has a list of the items in order. The representative returns to their group and draws the first word in picture form on the list. When someone guesses it they send up someone else to receive the next word on the list and they go back and draw it. The first team to finish the whole list wins.

Note

- You must explain carefully that when people race up to the leader for the next item on the list they must remember the previous one, otherwise, the leader won't know where the team is up to.

- You may wish to make it a rule that everyone in the group must have at least one or two turns. Otherwise you could find that the same person (who happens to be a good artist) hogs the whole game.

- There must be no cheating by the artist. He or she must not speak in any way. Be strict on this rule.

- A variation on this game is to play 'Scripture Picture Charades'. That is, the person in the group must act out the item on the list instead of drawing it!

5. Celebrity Tic Tac Toe

Nominate nine leaders or leaders and kids as 'celebrities'. Set up two rows of three chairs. The first three people sit on chairs in the first row, the next three people stand behind the first row of chairs and then next three stand on chairs behind them, forming a grid of nine celebrities. Like most games, there are two teams. Ask for a volunteer from a team to choose a celebrity. The celebrity is asked a question and can answer correctly or incorrectly. The team player has to agree or disagree with their answer. If the volunteer chooses correctly (they have agreed when the celebrity gave the correct answer and they have disagreed when the celebrity gave the incorrect answer) they take that square and the celebrity holds up either a nought or a cross (X or 0) depending on which team it is. First team with three celebrities in a row wins. A variation on this game is to have the celebrity ask a question. A volunteer chooses a celebrity. The celebrity asks the volunteer's team a question. If someone from the team answers it correctly, they win the square.

6. Celebrity Tic Tac Toe 2

On a blackboard/whiteboard or a large piece of paper draw a tic tac toe (noughts and crosses) grid. In each square you place a picture cut out of a magazine of someone famous. Behind the picture you place a number. The number corresponds with the number of the question you are going to ask from the Bible. Give each team either a nought or a cross (0 or X) or another symbol for their team. Each group, one at a time, picks a famous face. Ask them the question behind the face. If they give the right answer, they can place a cross or nought (or their team symbol) in the square. The first team to get three squares in a row is the winner.

7. Bible Challenge

The aim of Bible Challenge is to help the young people get to know their Bible better. It is especially good for kids who have little or no experience in handling the Bible. It will help them to become more familiar with it in a general way.

Divide the group into teams of two or three (or they can play individually). Ask the teams to sit down and give each team a Bible. Ask a question and the first group to put up their hands can answer. For each correct answer they receive a point for their team. The team with the most points at the end of the game is the winner.

Sample questions:

1. How many chapters in the book of Psalms? *150*

2. How many books in the Bible? *66*

3. Name a book in the Old Testament that starts with the letter E? *Exodus, Ezra, Esther, Ezekiel*

4. Name four books from the Old Testament that have boy's names. *Joshua, Samuel, Ezra, Nehemiah, Job, Isaiah, and any of the last 14 books of the Old Testament.*

5. Look up 1 John 1:5. What does it say? *This is the message we have heard from him and declare to you: God is light; in him there is no darkness at all.*

6. What is the first word in the Bible? *In*

7. How many books in the whole Bible start with the letter P? *6*

8. In the New Testament how many names of books begin with a number? *11*

9. How many verses in Luke 22? *71*

10. Name a book in the Old Testament that has a girl's name? *Ruth or Esther*

A variation on this game would be to have them answer on paper. Whatever you do, the game must move quickly.

8. Biblical Secret Sounds

This is like the secret sounds you may have heard on the radio. Pick a sound related to a Bible narrative and record it onto a tape (some examples are given below). Play the sound to your group a couple of times during the programme. You can give clues progressively to help them figure it out. You could also offer a prize such as a Mars Bar. If no one gets it that week, offer the Mars Bar and another chocolate as the award for next week. Let the game continue for a couple of weeks with the prize pool increasing each week. If no one guesses it, give bigger clues. You could tell them the name of the book it's in, hopefully this will encourage them to go home and read the book to find the secret sound.

Examples of different sounds:

1. The sound of scissors cutting (you could put in a wicked-sounding laugh as well), which would be Delilah having Samson's hair cut.

2. The sound of water pouring into cups would be Jesus turning water into wine.

3. The sound of a garage door closing and then the sound of the water coming from the hose against the door. This would be closing the door on the ark and the rain arriving.

4. The sound of pots and pans and other things crashing to the ground. Also the sound of money falling on the ground. This would be Jesus clearing the temple.

9. Biblical Secret Sounds Live!

Instead of taping a sound and playing it for the group, have the group break up into small groups or pairs. Ask them to come up with their own Biblical Secret Sound. They then present this to the group. If you can, have them stand behind something that hides them from the group (like an office partition, or a blanket draped on a couple of stacks of chairs). The group tries to guess the sound.

10. Cryptic Biblical Secret Sounds

Instead of sounds that are designed to be a straight reproduction of a sound that could be in the Bible, give it a cryptic twist. For instance, you could a have a telephone ringing with a man answering it. This could be God calling Abram in Genesis. This will take some thinking on your part, but it is a lot of fun.

11. Bible 'Freeze Frames'

Divide the group into pairs, triplets or small groups. Give them a few minutes to plan a scene from the Bible, which they will present to the rest of the group as a still or picture. The group then tries to guess which scene from the Bible they are portraying. If it helps, allow them to have one movement (a second still shot). In other words, they set the scene or picture, and then are allowed one slight movement to help the group guess what it is they are acting out. For instance, you could have a boy with his arms stretched out and a girl standing next to him. The movement would be her reaching up to grab something from his hands. This scene would be Eve eating the fruit from the tree of the knowledge of good and evil.

12. Props

Break the group into smaller groups. Give each group one or more 'props'. These can be either simple household items or more unusual items. The goal is for each group to come up with as many stories from the Bible as they can that has the prop in it. They then briefly act the stories out. For example, if you gave a group a large spoon, they could act out a number scenes that deal with cooking in the Bible (Genesis 25:29 Jacob and Esau; Luke 10: 38-41 Martha and Mary). The rest of the group tries to guess the story they are acting out. You could even award points for the best drama or the most scenes done in a given time (two minutes). You could give them a special award if they can act out the scenes in the order they occur in the Bible.
(Thanks to Phil vant Spyker from Northmead Anglican Church for this idea.)

13. True or False

The group is standing while the person running the game makes a series of statements. Each person in the group must decide if they think the statement is true or false. If it is true they put their hands on their heads; if it is false then they put their hands on their 'tails'. After you have revealed the answer, the people who had the wrong answer sit down. Continue until there is a winner.

Alternatively, everyone stands in the middle of the room. Mark the two ends of the room True and False – if they think the statement you make is true, they run to the end of the room marked true, if they think it is false, they go to the other.

A variation of this game is to divide into two teams, for instance, boys versus girls, and the first person to run to the correct side wins a point for their team. To prevent cheating, deduct a point from the team that runs to the wrong side first.

You can use this game to illustrate any statement of the gospel – in this postmodern world it is good to challenge people's belief that a statement can be either true or false and they have to decide: there is no middle ground. For example, Jesus is God – True or false.

14. Bible Blanks

Divide the group into two teams. Give each person a piece of paper and a pencil. This game is made up of various 'rounds'. In each round, ask for a volunteer from each team. This person is the 'contestant'. Send the two contestants to another part of the room, perhaps the other end of the hall (we call ours the 'sound proof booth'). The leader reads out a statement with a missing word (blank), such as, '_____ is a book in the New Testament'. Each person, including the contestants, writes down what he or she thinks the missing word could be. For instance, the person who has volunteered could write 'Matthew'. The contestants then rejoin the group (coming up to the front) and each in turn reveals what their word is. As they do this, everyone in the team displays the word they have written (one team at a time). The aim of the game is for each person in the group to have the same word as the 'contestant'. Each team gets 10 points for each answer that is the same. To spice things up you can have double and triple point rounds.

Sample statements:

1. The name of a woman in the Old Testament is _____ (They are to write down the name of a female in the Old Testament such as Eve, Sarah or Rebekah)

2. _____ was one of Jesus' disciples.

3. We always do _____ at youth group.

4. One of Jesus' miracles was _____.

5. _____ was one of the many books that Paul wrote.

6. One of our youth group leaders is called _____.

Note

It is crucial that no one shouts out an answer or even mutters it under his or her breath. It is also important that team members do not speak to each other in the hope of coming up with the same answer.

15. Bible Match

Put the names of characters in the Bible on cards and different events or people associated with these characters on other cards, for example, Moses on one card and the Ten commandments on another. Have around 20 cards and place them up on the wall or on the floor in rows (five cards going across and four going down, with the writing facing the wall or floor). Obviously you won't put the matching cards next to each other, they should be scattered over the grid. Divide the group into two teams and, one at a time, each team chooses two cards to turn over. If they make a match, award a point to the team. If they don't match the cards, they need to remember what cards are where, so that when the matching partner comes up, they remember where it can be found. Then it is the next team's turn and so on until all the cards are matched up. The aim is for the young people to link people and events in the Bible.

Examples

Old Testament characters and events
Daniel – the Lion's Den
Moses – 10 Commandments
Rehoboam – division of the Kingdom of Israel
Noah – Ark
Adam and Eve – Garden of Eden
David – Goliath
Joshua – walls of Jericho tumbling down
Ezra – Rebuilding the Temple
Ehud – stabbing of Eglon king of Moab
Nehemiah – Rebuilding Israel's city walls
Samson – killed many more when he died than while he lived

New Testament characters and events
Peter – denied knowing Jesus
Judas – betrayal
Saul – Road to Damascus
Lydia – Philippi

Friends
David – Jonathan
Paul – Timothy

Paul – Mark

Family
Rachel – Leah
Jacob – Esau
Moses – Aaron
David – Solomon
Joseph – Benjamin
James – John
Ruth – Naomi
Mordecai – Esther
Cain – Seth
Ham – Shem
Mary – Elizabeth
Jesus – John the Baptist
Abraham – Lot
Hagar – Ishmael
Abraham – Sarah
Adam – Eve
Cain – Abel
Mary – Joseph
Moses – Miriam
Jacob – Leah
Jacob – Rachel

16. Head Buzzer Game

Divide the group into teams (boys versus girls, or various school years against each other – year 7 versus year 8. The more teams the better). Two people represent each group; one person is the 'player' (who answers questions) and one person is the 'buzzer'. Each buzzer sits on a chair and the player stands behind them. When a question is asked, the players indicate that they want to answer by pressing their 'buzzer' on the head (gently). When they press the 'buzzer's head, the buzzer calls out their team name (for example, if the team is year/grade 7, the buzzer calls out 'year 7' when his or her head is pressed). It is a good idea to have a 'half time' when the buzzer and player swap positions with each other. The team that answers the most questions wins.

The Head Buzzer game is best played when coupled with another Bible quiz game such as *Fill in the Blanks*. If the group is large, you can use it with noughts and crosses where representatives from that team in the crowd take a position on a noughts and crosses board. To play this you need only two teams (boys vs girls or year 7-8 vs year 9).
(Thanks to All Saints, Anglican Church, Lindfield, Sydney for this idea.)

17. Draw your 'swords' (Ephesians 6:17)

This game helps people to find their way around the Bible. Everybody places their closed Bible (their sword) under their arm. The leader reads out a Bible reference and everybody pulls out their Bible and looks up the reference. When they find it they stand up. The first person to stand is the winner, who then reads out the verse. You can do this at different times throughout your programme and you can do it through the talk when you need verses looked up. (It's actually a lot of fun.)

18. 66 Books of the Bible review

This is to help the group learn the books of the Bible. Divide your group into two or more teams (have three or four people in each group). Give the teams a few minutes to work together to come up with the names of as many books of the Bible as they can remember. Have one team begin with someone naming one of the books (they don't have to be in order). The next team has someone stand and name a different book of the Bible. The game continues with the teams taking it in turn to give the name of a book. When a team gets a name wrong or they have run out of names they are out of the game. The game keeps going until there is only one team left.

19. Poison Ball / Protect the Truth

You may have played an old game called 'poison ball'. There are two teams at opposite ends of the hall, each with a ball. The object is to throw the ball at members of the opposing team and if they are hit below the knee they are out of the game. To give this game a nice twist, someone on each team is nominated to be 'The Truth'. The other team members have to protect 'The Truth' without revealing who it is to the other team. If the person nominated 'The Truth' is hit, the whole team is out. Therefore it is in the interest of each team member to sacrifice him or herself by being hit with the ball to prevent it hitting 'The Truth'. Otherwise, the whole team loses. The first team to hit 'The Truth' wins.

This is a more energetic game and is a classic case of taking a straw game which doesn't do much more than burn up energy, and with a bit of thought, changing it to give it a positive message. A game like this should be linked to the message that will be given later on (for instance if you were doing a study on 2 Timothy 1:14).
(Thanks to Seven Hills Anglican Church in Sydney for this idea.)

Now it's your turn!

Be creative and develop new Bible games

This world needs more Bible games! Think. Spend time discussing and brainstorming with your leaders. Start developing games that your group can play for years to come.

Tell Ken when you devise a new game (kjmoser@hotmail.com)

We are always on the lookout for new games. If you come up with one, let us know and we'll take the credit and hog the glory. Umm, I mean we will make sure we pass it on to others so they can play it as well.

C H A P T E R 5

Memory Verses

Key thought:	Learn Bible verses or passages in a fun and helpful way.
Reflection:	Do the young people in your group know their Bible? Are they able to recall Scripture verses that tell them what Jesus has done for them? Can they use the 'sword of the Spirit' when they face difficult times? Can they remember Bible verses when they are talking to their friends about Jesus?

All Scripture is God-breathed and is useful for teaching, rebuking, correcting and training in righteousness, so that the man of God may be thoroughly equipped for every good work. (2 Timothy 3:16,17)

Take the helmet of salvation and the sword of the Spirit, which is the word of God. (Ephesians 6:17)

We all want to see the young people in our groups come to know and love God's word. This will go a long way toward giving them confidence about sharing the good news of

Jesus with friends and family. Knowing the word of God also reminds us of how we are to live in a way that pleases God. For example, when we are tempted to do the wrong thing, God's word will remind us that we are to say 'no' to temptation and encourage us to remain faithful to God.

A great addition to any youth group programme is a segment for memorising a verse or a passage from scripture. If it is boring and tedious, forget it. You must do it well and make it fun. In our youth group we take a verse (or verses) and run with it for three weeks. By the end of that time most of the group have a fair understanding and recall of the verse. (We also print the verse on a small card for each member of the group.) Memory verse time has become one of the highlights of our weekly gathering.

Helpful ways to lead memory verse segments

Choose good verses

Choose Bible verses that will be helpful for the group. Spend a couple of months on verses about the good news of Jesus such as 1 John 4:10: John 3:16; Mark 10:45 and Romans 6:23. (These are also helpful for telling nonChristians about what it means to be a Christian.) After this, move on to verses that point out what this means for us (2 Corinthians 5:17; Galatians 2:20; Ephesians 2:8,9 and 1 John 3:1). You can then spend a few months on verses helpful to living the Christian life (Philippians 1:21; James 1:22; 1 John 1:8,9 and 1 John 4:7). The whole process is designed to give the young people in your group a growing knowledge of Christ and confidence in talking to those who don't know him. (There is a list of helpful memory verses in the Resource section on page 125.)

Make sure the group has time to learn the verses

Do not run the Memory Verse segment for one week and then skip it for a few weeks. Spend at least three weeks on each verse. Your goal is to drive it home and have the group learn it for life. The pattern I would suggest is to introduce the verse (week one), revise and remember the verse (week two) and review the verse (week three).

To introduce the verse, you could use a game like *Fill in the Blanks* or *Human Buzzer*. To revise and remember, you could form small groups and do skits. To review the verse, you could have someone from the group recite the verse. You could then write it up on a whiteboard and then ask volunteers to stand up and recite the verse as you slowly rub letters and words off the board.

At my youth group, after we have introduced the verse by way of a game, one of the leaders stands up and says the verse a number of times (usually in a funny or crazy way). The group then repeats it after him phrase by phrase, imitating him.

Make sure you learn where the verse comes from as well. Often groups learn the verse but forget to learn the reference!

Give out 'memory verse cards'

An effective way to help the group learn the verse is to hand out a printed card with the verse on it. These are available at most Christian bookshops. You will find that the selection is limited so it's best to make your own. Enlist the aid of someone in your group who is a whizz with a computer and will easily be able to print out cards with verses on them.

Use memory verse questions in your Bible game questions

Memory verses can make great subjects for questions in your Bible games. The more verses you learn, the more questions you can use in a review. For instance, if you have learned Mark 10:45, (For even the Son of Man did not come to be served, but to serve, and to give his life as a ransom for many). You can ask questions such as, 'Where does the Bible speak of the Son of Man coming and giving his life as a ransom for many'? (*Answer:* Mark 10:45). Or you could ask, 'Which Bible verse tells us about the ransom that Jesus paid?' You could give them a hint such as, 'It was one of our memory verses a month or so ago.' Using questions based on memory verses will help your group to remember them.

Make this a regular part of your programme. Learning memory verses is good for everybody in the group, nonChristian and Christian alike. Even kids who are there for the first time can be blessed through learning a verse from the Bible. It will also send a signal that the group takes God's word seriously.

Be creative

Like any other part of your programme, memory verses can become stale if you fall into a rut. Spend time as a leadership team thinking through new ideas and ways to have fun learning new verses.

HOT TIP A great way to do a memory verse is to enlist the support of some of the kids in your group. Take a few of the keen kids aside and explain to them that in a couple of weeks you need them to run a memory verse for three weeks in a row. Tell them that you want something fun and creative. See what they come up with. Hopefully, they will be excited and take the job seriously. It should also be a lot of fun for the group. It may also lead others in the group to come up with new ideas.

Link Bible games with the memory verse

There are a number of Bible games that can be based on your memory verse. Games like *Letter by Letter* or *Human Buzzer* work well.

Final thought

The Memory verse segment is a time where the group remembers the great things in God's word. It is a chance to hit the target of having a time together that is Christian, group building and a lot of fun. Don't use any of the ideas below if they aren't appropriate for your group.

Over 20 creative ways to learn memory verses

1. Do the verse in various 'styles'

Whoever is teaching or leading the verse can say it in a certain style and the group has to mimic him or her. For instance, you could do it homeboy[1], cartoon characters, famous actors, youth leaders, cowboys, and foreign accents.

2. Sing it

Form into small groups and 'perform' the verse in various styles. Give each group a different singing style such as opera, country and western, rock and roll. Give the group time to work out how they will sing it and then each group has to sing the memory verse in their style for the rest of the meeting.

3. Fill in the Blanks

(See chapter four on Bible Games for a description of the game.)

4. First letter revision

Write the memory verse in blanks with the first letter of each word attached, for example:

F_ _ t_ m_, t_ l_ _ _ i_ C_ _ _ _ _ a_ _ t_ d_ _ i_ g_ _ _.
_ _ _ _ _ _ _ _ _ _ _ _ _ _ _:_ _

(For to me, to live is Christ and to die is gain. Philippians 1:21)

There are several ways to reveal the memory verse:

- You could divide the group into two teams and ask a series of Bible questions and with each correct answer they fill out one word. Continue until someone is able to quote the whole verse. (Like *Fill in the Blanks* – see Bible games.)

- You could form small groups and give each group a piece of paper. The first letters of each word of the verse can be written up on the board or on the sheet itself. Give each group a certain amount of time (2–5 minutes) to complete the verse. The winner is the group with the most complete verse.

---

1. I think a Homeboy is someone who likes rap music, wears baggy pants and his cap backwards. Personally, I listen to Bruce Springsteen and wear Levi's.

5. Memory Verse Circle

Your group sits in a circle on chairs. Give each person one or two words (or phrases) of the memory verse so that the whole verse, including the reference (chapter and verse) is given to all the people sitting in the circle.

Ask each person to recite the word (or words) given in order, so the whole memory verse is recited. You can do this a couple of times seeing how fast they can complete the verse.

Then tell everyone to move a number of seats in the same direction (for instance, move three seats to their left). However, their word/s stays with the seat, so they have to find out the word/s from the person who was sitting in that seat before.

Ask everyone to say the new word or words in order. Do this a couple of times. Have the group change seat a few more times until people are really learning the verse. A fun twist is to have everyone close their eyes when they say it. Or, you could add a 'Mexican Wave'. When each person says their word, they must either stand or raise their hands.

After a couple of times of doing this, see if someone can stand up and say the verse alone.

A fun addition is to have someone with a stopwatch time the group. Set a time (say 10 seconds) and see if the group can do it faster than the set time.

(With a very large group you may need to form several smaller groups for the exercise to work well.)

6. Throw an object

Check to see if anyone remembers the verse. Whoever remembers, stands up and recites it. Sit in a circle and give one person an item to throw (such as a tennis ball). The person with the ball says the first word of the memory verse and then randomly throws the ball to someone else. The person receiving the ball says the next word of the memory verse and throws it to someone else, and so on until the verse is completed with verse reference. You can play this until the verse is repeated successfully three times with no errors or after a practice run, you can begin to eliminate people until you have one person left who then has to recite the whole verse.

Note: With some groups, you must make a rule to throw the ball *to* the person and not *at* the person. Failure to comply means elimination from the game.

(If you have a very large group you may need to break up into a couple of smaller groups for the exercise to work.)

7. Word for Word Relay

Check to see if anyone remembers the verse, and if someone does, ask the person to stand up and recite it. Divide the group into two teams. Give each team a whiteboard marker (or chalk) and as a race against the other team, each person has to run to the board and write one word of the memory verse in order. Once they have written their word, they run back to their team and give the pen to another person who writes the next word on the board and so on. The winner is the first team to finish word perfect with reference.

It's a lot of fun as people try to remember what word comes next and they work as a team to remember each word. For a shorter verse, you could make it more difficult by having them write a letter at a time.

Variation: for groups of 4 or less people

Give each person a different coloured marker pen. Review the verse so that people can remember it. Ask each person in turn a Bible question. If they get the right answer they write up a word of the memory verse starting from the beginning of the verse. The winner is the person with the most words in their colour of pen.
(Thanks to Sarah from Auburn Anglican for this idea.)

8. Characters

A leader stands on a chair out the front. The leader takes on a character from a television show (such as 'The Simpsons') or some other fun, crazy style. The leader recites the memory verse phrase by phrase speaking and doing whatever actions are appropriate. The group (which is also standing) repeats the leader's words and actions after each phrase, copying the way the leader spoke and doing the same actions.

If the leader is not confident to do this well, another option is to have a young person stand on a chair, the leader recites the verse phrase by phrase (in a normal voice). The young person on the chair copies the leader's words, however, he or she adds the character voices/actions etc. and the group needs to imitate the young person. This is often a better model as the group hears each phrase of the verse twice before they repeat it.

9. Mirrors

The person leading the memory verse stands in front of the group and says the verse with actions. The group then mimics the actions as they say the verse. If possible, the actions should in some way reflect the words of the verse.

10. Jigsaw puzzle

Write out the memory verse on a large piece of cardboard and cut it into jigsaw pieces. Then have the group put the jigsaw back together. This would be played the second or third week of the memory verse when the verse is familiar to them. With a larger group, have more than one puzzle and make it a competition to see which team finishes first.

11. Jigsaw puzzle 2

Write down the memory verse on a large sheet of paper. Cut up the paper into a number of smaller pieces and tape them under the chairs in your meeting place before the young people enter. When the time is right, tell the young people to look under their seats, then stand and form a line in the correct order of the verse. Depending on the number of people in your group, you can either divide the verse into separate words or phrases or even divide the words into syllables. Once the group is in line you can have them say the verse in order.

12. Drama

Form into small groups and have each group act out the memory verse in their own way or using a theme you give them. They could either act out the meaning of the verse or they could play on some of the words in the verse. Make sure they recite the verse in some fashion so that the group learns it.

Example

> If you were using Philippians 1:21: 'For to me, to live is Christ and to die is gain'. You could have a group act out each word in a line. Or, you could have them act out the meaning in a serious or humorous way.

If it is the first week of learning a verse, you could also ask the group to act out different words and what they mean from the memory verse. For example 'I am not ashamed of the gospel, because it is the power of God for the salvation of everyone who believes' Romans 1:16. They could act the words, ashamed, gospel, power, salvation, believes. Each group has a different word to demonstrate.

This method helps the group understand what the verse is about (which is just as important as learning it!).

Example

> We were learning Hebrews 9:27–28 as our memory verse. If you look it up in your Bible you'll see that it is quite long. We decided to spend three weeks on verse 27 alone. The verse reads, 'Just as man is destined to die once, and after that to face judgement'. The first week we did it the 'Fill in Blanks' style followed by skits designed to drive it home. The problem was, I wrote up the verse on the whiteboard and, in my hieroglyphic-like handwriting, some of the words were hard to read. It was at this stage that a couple of the girls got the giggles. I couldn't understand why until it came time to do the skits. The word 'die' looked to them like 'dip'. So, they did a skit about men double dipping their potato chips at a party and then facing judgment from the rest of the guests. It was a complete crack up. While it was a bit of a goof up on my part, in the end it was a success. The girls learned Hebrews 9:27 and will probably never forget it!

Numbers/nouns/verbs

This game is a bit more work but it is a lot of fun. Break your memory verse into nouns, verbs and any word that is either a number or resembles a number (for example 'to' or 'too'). Assign a word group to various subgroups within your group (boys/girls; age groups etc.). For example, Philippians 1:21: 'For to me, to live is Christ and to die is gain' contains the words 'for' and 'to' which sound like the numbers 4 and 2. These can go to one group, which must stand up and say the words that are like numbers. They would also say the numbers of the actual verse itself when it comes to saying the reference at the end. Another group would say the nouns and the verbs (me, live, is, Christ, die, is, gain, Philippians). Each time their word comes up, the group stands and says it and then sits down. The aim is to do it as fast as possible.

Example

> We did this with 1 Peter 3:18, 'For Christ died for sins once for all, the righteous for the unrighteous, to bring you to God.' We formed our group into three—one group took any word that is, or sounds like a number (for, for, once, for all, for, to, to). Another group said any word that was a noun (Christ, sins, righteous, unrighteous, you, God). The leaders spoke the verbs (died, bring). It was loud, active and good fun.

With harder or longer verses, form your group into more subgroups (not just two) and give them various categories (such as people, prepositions). It will help if you write it on an overhead or on a whiteboard.

14. Memory verse statues

Form into groups and act out the verse by making a statue or series of statues. If you were doing Philippians 1:21, you could have people raising four fingers, ('for') followed by two fingers ('to'). The next person points to him or herself ('me') and so on, down the line.

15. Words in balloons

Put each word of the memory verse in different balloons. Ask the group members to blow them up. Then as many volunteers as there are balloons burst them and try to put together the memory verse.

This can be done as a time trial with teams competing against each other.

You can have balloons tied around ankles with string. Two competing teams burst the balloons with their feet as quickly as possible and then organise the words into the order of the verse. Be careful with this one, don't let it get out of hand.

16. Basketball

Check to see if anyone remembers the verse. Ask whoever remembers it to stand up and recite it. Divide into two teams, each team has their own ball, which they throw into a garbage bin or basketball hoop. Each time they throw the ball they recite a word from the memory verse starting with the first word, until they get the ball in the basket for that word. If they miss the basket, they pass the ball to the next person. They cannot move on to the next word until the ball has been sunk for that word. If someone makes the basket they have another turn, moving on to the next word in the verse. The person can continue to throw until they miss. The winner is the first team to get to the end of the verse.

17. Blindfolds

Check to see if anyone remembers the verse, and if someone does, ask them to stand up and recite it. Allocate a word of the memory verse to everyone in the group, including the verse reference. You may have to give some people two or three words together if the verse is long or if there are not enough people. Hand a blindfold to each person. They then line up out of order of the verse, put on their blindfolds and rearrange themselves so that the verse is in order. Once finished they take off the blindfolds and recite the words – hopefully in the right order.

18. Pass the Parcel

Played like the game 'Pass the Parcel'. Wrap a prize (usually a bar of chocolate) in a piece of paper with part of a memory verse on it and so on. The group sits in a circle, play music and when the music stops, the person holding the package removes a layer to receive a word or a part of the memory verse. Make sure the verse is in random order. When the last piece is uncovered, the whole group puts together the verse, including the verse reference.
(Thanks to Gladesville Anglican church for this idea.)

19. Word Relay

Write different parts of a verse (either individual words or phrases) on pieces of paper and stick them on the wall around the room, randomly placed. Divide the group into two teams. It is a relay race and each member has to go to the pieces in order. For example the first team member of each group runs to the first word of the verse, touches it and then runs back to their team and tips the second person who runs to the second word of the verse until the whole verse is completed. When the verse is completed the group shouts out the memory verse (with reference) and the first team to finish wins.
(Thanks to Gladesville Anglican church.)

A variation of this is to have the memory verse printed on pieces of paper and scattered around the hall. Form the group into teams. The goal is to collect all the words and put them in correct order. The winner is the first team to do so. (The number of teams will dictate how many copies of the verse you scatter around the hall. For instance two teams – two copies of the verse. You can print the verse in various colours. One colour per team.)

20. Memory verse scavenger hunt

Divide the group into teams. Give them a list of clues. These clues are designed to lead them to a 'secret location'. At each location is a part of the memory verse. For example, if your church has a stairway or steps, the first clue could be 'Stairway to Heaven'. Under the steps (or taped to the side) could be part of the memory verse. The group then proceeds to the next clue to retrieve another part of the verse. The winner is the first group to collect all parts of the verse. Two things: this game takes a bit of preparation and, you may need to set up two or three different sets of clue locations. This will prevent groups following each other or trying to sabotage the game.

21. Memory Verse Challenge

This would be a review game to play at the end of the year or end of term. It reviews all the memory verses the group has learned. Form the group into two or more teams. Give the teams a few minutes to work together to come up with as many of the memory verses as they can remember. Ask one team to begin with someone saying one of the memory verses they have learnt. It has to be close to word perfect for it to be correct. When they have finished, someone from the next team stands up and says another memory verse word perfect. When a team is unable to continue, they drop out. The game keeps going until there is only one team left. (There will no doubt be one person in your group who has learned most of the verses. To prevent them monopolising the game, it may be helpful to set a rule that someone different has to stand up each time and recite the verse.) A variation of this would be to give paper and pens to each group and ask them to write down all the memory verses they can remember in five to ten minutes. The winner is the team with the most verses.

C H A P T E R   6

Question and Answer Times (Q+A)

Key thought:	Young people often have questions. Spend some time in your weekly gathering trying to answer them. Q&A is about helping young people to grow more like Jesus, not just to convey facts.
Reflection:	Is there a time in your group for the young people to ask or discuss questions? Is youth group a place where people feel comfortable about asking big questions?

Young people have questions. It's their nature. Youth group must provide a safe environment where they can ask their questions and receive good, solid Christian answers. A regular Q&A is a helpful segment to have in your programme. You may find that this takes a week or so to get going, but once it does it should become a very helpful part of your programme. (You may wish to give it a more appropriate name. We call ours Q&A, but that's because we couldn't think of anything better.)

Example

When we introduced Q&A to our present youth group we expected to be confronted with muffled silence. We assumed that the young people wouldn't have any questions the first time around. (We have found this is what usually happens – week one we introduce it, no response – we then tell the group that 'we will do it again next week, so come prepared'. Quite often, it takes a few attempts to really succeed.) We were surprised to be asked one question straight away. We spent some time on that question and there were no more questions from the group. We told them we would 'do it again next week'. The next week I was a little nervous as to whether it would succeed. I explained what Q&A was, and then asked if there were any questions. One young man put his hand in the air and said, 'I have 17 questions!' He then reached in his back pocket, pulled out a piece of paper and said, 'Number one; does the Bible ...'. Needless to say I was blown away. We never looked back after that. These days it is not unusual for us to have a Q&A that lasts 15 minutes.

Guidelines for running a Q&A:

Be prepared

The person running Q&A must be prepared to lead and equipped either to answer questions or hand them over to another leader or expert. There are several ways to run Q&A (see below). The leader must be clear about how to run this segment and what he/she hopes to achieve. Do not be sloppy or unprepared.

Set the tone

Do not stand up and say, 'Alright, you probably have questions about God and stuff. Who has a question?' If you do this, almost certainly you will be greeted by deafening silence. The leader must stand up and announce that there is going to be a question time. That is, a time to field any questions people in the group might have. My line is, 'You may have a question about God, the Bible or being a Christian. You may have heard something that confused you. Or, you may have been asked a question by your teacher or friend that you couldn't answer. You may even have read something in the Bible that has confused you. While I may not be able to answer every question, I'll give it a shot. If I can't answer it here, I'll try to find the answer during the week and we'll discuss it next week.' Then I repeat what we are doing and why. I give the kids a few seconds to think and then invite them to ask their questions.

Be Patient

When you are standing in front of a group, time has a sneaky way of going weird. Long times can feel short, and short times can feel like an eternity. My practice is that after I have asked if there are any questions, I count backwards from ten in my head (don't let the group hear you, they'll think you're nuts!). If there are no questions I repeat, 'You may have a question about God, the Bible or being a Christian. You may have heard something that confused you. Or, you may have been asked a question by your teacher or friend that you couldn't answer. You may even have read something in the Bible that confused you. Now is a time to ask and see if we can find an answer.' Usually a question arises. If not, let them know that you will be doing it again next week and then move on to another part of the programme.

Promote good relationships

The more comfortable young people are with the group, the better this will succeed. If the young people do not feel safe or there is a spirit of harsh joking and criticism, they will never open up and admit that they have questions. Make sure you are doing things that promote good relationships in the group.

No fake questions

I once ran a Q&A where the group had no questions. It wasn't panic time, as I didn't feel the group was hostile nor did they seem disinterested. They genuinely looked as if at that moment in time there was nothing they could think of to ask. Suddenly, one leader, seeking to help, raised his hand and said, 'Tell us Ken, why did Jesus die on that cross?' It was an awkward moment. Everyone knew that this was not an authentic question. While his intentions were good, the group realised that this was a set up. Avoid this. If there are no questions, don't force it. Move on.

Don't force questions

Do not abuse the group if they don't ask anything. This is quite common. The leader realises that there are no questions and begins to panic. Instead of calmly inviting questions, he challenges the group with statements like, 'So, you know everything do you?' Or, 'What, cat got your tongue?' Kids should ask questions if they feel comfortable. Do not force them into asking questions if they don't want to.

Give plenty of time to think

The leader of the Q&A must feel comfortable with silence while the group spends a moment reflecting on whether or not they have any questions. Once, I saw a leader get up and say, 'Ok guys, it's Q&A time. Any questions?' In about the time it took to blink, he said, 'No? Oh well that went well didn't it?' He then sat down. The whole episode took about 10 seconds! Give them time. Don't panic and run it like a Formula One Grand Prix.

Avoid the 'question box'

The question box is designed to make asking questions easier. While the question box has a positive side, it also has a downside. One of your goals is to run your youth group in a way that promotes community and a sense of 'we are a group'. You hope to run a group where kids feel comfortable enough to share openly and honestly. You want a group where questions can be asked without fear or embarrassment. A box for questions depersonalises the whole process. Boxes say to the group, 'Some of you are scared, here is an easy option'. If you feel that the group is not ready to openly share questions, work at creating an atmosphere that will overcome this fear before introducing Q&A.

Note

If you are committed to the question box because you feel it provides a 'safe forum' for questions, doubts etc, think about using your youth group's website. If your group doesn't have a website, ask one of the kids to set one up. These days it is simple and cheap to do. Once there is a website, a part of the site can be devoted to Q&A. You can then bring the questions to the next youth meeting and this can be the start of your Q&A. This is a more modern version of the old question box.

Run Q&A for a couple of weeks in a row

If Q&A takes off you may find that there are some weeks where you run out of time. If this is the case, plan on running it a couple of weeks in a row.

Tips on answering questions

It can be tough to stand up in front of a group and try to answer questions 'off the cuff'. Therefore, be prepared.

1. Always affirm the question. The leader should say, 'That's a good question.' Never belittle a question or the questioner. This reply will also give you a moment to reflect on the question and not immediately launch into an answer.

2. Don't give a full-scale thesis of detailed Biblical Theology starting with hyper supralapsarianism and finishing with a post tribulational premillennianism, when all the kid wants to know is whether animals go to heaven! Keep answers as simple as possible. Also, realise that you are dealing with 12–16 year olds. Try to think like them and give an answer that is true and appropriate.

3. It is often helpful to allow a number of questions on the same topic. Once you have given an answer, invite the young person to come back with a related question or make a comment on your answer. For instance, if someone asks about whether animals go to heaven, this may lead to a number of related questions and maybe even a lively group discussion. This can be a great thing. Encourage it! Often I will say, 'Did I answer your question? Does anyone else want to make a comment or ask a question on that topic before we move on?'

4. Always seek to discover the 'question behind the question'. For instance, if someone asks about forgiveness, it may because they are dealing with guilt and fear of judgment. Be gentle but try to be wise and seek to answer the real question. Q&A is about helping young people to grow more like Jesus, not just convey facts.

5. It is helpful to answer questions with a personal example. If they ask you about drinking alcohol at parties, it may be helpful to have some leaders briefly talk about the situations they have faced and how they responded in a way that honours God.

6. Be prepared beforehand to take questions on topics that are likely to arise – alcohol, sex, parents, and God's sovereignty will almost always make an appearance. Be prepared. (See Hot Tip on page 83–84 of *Changing the World*.)

7. Finally, it is OK not to know all the answers. Young people have a way of asking questions that you didn't even know existed! It is not a disgrace to scratch your head and say, 'Wow, that is a really good question. I'll have to come back to you on that one.' Do some homework during the week and try to answer it at the next meeting.

If Q&A doesn't succeed immediately, stay with it! Youth group is about finding life in Christ and growing in knowledge of him with his people. Question and answer times can be a great help to young people seeking to make big decisions about life. If it doesn't take off right away, keep trying. If it falls flat, smile and ask again, 'Are there any question? No? We'll see if there are any in a week or two!' Then move on. If the leader is comfortable and relaxed, the kids will soon understand that this is a great thing and go with you.

Seven ways to run Q&A:

The Classic

A leader stands up and explains what happens, gives the group time to think and then seeks to answer any questions from the group.

The 'Share a question with the person next to you'

Quite often the driving force for a young person is not to look stupid. Even though they may have a burning question, they won't admit it if they are fearful of what the group will think. Therefore, make it easy for them! The leader stands up and explains that Q&A is an opportunity for them to have their questions answered. However, instead of taking questions classic style, the leader says 'turn to the person next to you (or the friend they are sitting with) and share with them any relevant questions.' The group then spends some time chatting and talking and hopefully sharing any questions. The kids will probably find that the person next to them often has the same question! This may be a little more comfortable for them than getting up the courage to ask a question in front of the group. After a minute or two the leader asks, 'What questions did you come up with? Who will share one with the group?' You should find that this leads to a fruitful question time. This has worked well (especially if you are a bit hesitant about launching straight into the 'classic').

The Expert

Tell the group that a special guest will be coming to take questions the following week. This person can be someone who is generally good at answering questions, or can be an expert in certain areas (the Old Testament, cults, creation and evolution etc.). This will prepare the group for next week's Q&A. It may be a good idea for the guest to give a short 2–5 minute talk on the subject to warm up the group. Similarly, you could organise a panel to take questions. I have done this with a group of parents who were there to field questions on parenting, and how to get along with your parents. It worked well.

Shout & write

Explain Q&A, but instead of taking questions one at a time, take them rapid fire as kids shout them out. Take the questions quickly, maybe even with kids shouting them out randomly. Someone quickly writes them down on an overhead sheet or on a whiteboard. After the questions die down, begin to answer them one by one. This is a rowdy way of doing it, so make sure you and your group can cope.

Q&A sheets

Prepare a sheet beforehand on which each member of the group can jot down any questions that crop up during the week. If you are able, remind the group during the week to remember to fill out these sheets when a question arises and to bring them to the next youth group meeting (you could remind them if you see them in small group Bible study or by mail). This may bring about a fruitful Q&A.

Group Wisdom

We have added a variation to the standard Q&A. Sometimes there are people in the group who are confronted with a problem that is difficult for them to figure out. We provide a time in youth group to share the problem and see if anyone in the group can provide a helpful solution or suggestion. The way we do this is simple. Either we provide a time in the weekly meeting for people in the group to share their question or problem. The group then tries to help them. Or, if an individual seeks out a leader privately and raises an issue or problem, the leader then asks if this problem can be raised anonymously in front of the group. This is done only with problems that aren't of a highly serious or confidential nature.

Wisdom Spot

In a similar vein, it may be helpful to add a segment called 'Wisdom Spot'. Have the group memorise James 1:5 as a memory verse ('If any of you lacks wisdom he should ask God who gives generously to all without finding fault'). You can then have a time where anyone in the group needing wisdom can bring their question or situation before the group. You can have a time of prayer for them asking God to give them wisdom. You could also see if anyone has a helpful answer or suggestion.

How to run Q&A

Step 1: Decide who will run it.

Step 2: Decide what style you will use.

Step 3: Stand up, introduce it and give the group time to think of any questions they might have.

Step 4: Take questions and try to answer them.

Step 5: If it is appropriate, seek to have a group discussion on any of the topics raised.

CHAPTER 7

Testimonies ... Testify!

Key thought:	It can be a great encouragement to hear how God has worked or is working in a person's life. It is also a great witness to nonChristians.
Reflection:	Are the young people in your group regularly hearing others tell how they became followers of Christ? Is your youth group a place where time is devoted to healthy sharing about what Christ has done/is doing in people's lives? Are the young people encouraged to speak about their walk with God? If a new person comes to the group, do they hear about the living God who is at work in people's lives?

But encourage one another daily, as long as it is called Today, so that none of you may be hardened by sin's deceitfulness (Hebrews 3:13).

Let us not give up meeting together, as some are in the habit of doing, but let us encourage one another — and all the more as you see the Day approaching (Hebrews 10:25).

A testimony is a great part of the programme. It is encouraging and challenging to hear how someone became a Christian. It is also an encouragement for the group to hear about what God is doing in each person's life. Testimonies will also show nonChristians in your group that God is alive and ready for a relationship with them. Make testimonies and testifying a regular part of your programme. We have two segments devoted to this. We call testimonies I.T.T. or 'Impromptu Testimony Time'. This is a chance for members of the group to stand up and give their testimony 'off the cuff'. We also have a time to testify when people tell the group about something special that God has done for them lately.

Some helpful guidelines

Testimonies are about Jesus

There is a temptation to spend more time talking about ourselves and our former life of crime than the grace of God found in Christ. When we testify, we are telling others about God, not ourselves. While we must obviously spend some time talking about ourselves, make sure that Jesus gets the spotlight!

Keep it short!

Testimonies should be brief. It may be helpful to have a leader stand at the front with the young people giving the testimony, just in case they begin to tell their entire life story rather than how they became a Christian.

Set up a 'culture of testifying'

For the first few weeks of the year, or, before introducing a testimony segment to your programme, have your leaders give their testimonies. Have one leader each week talk about how they became a Christian. If there is a shortage of leaders, invite trustworthy members of your congregation to come and give their testimony. Either way, you want youth group to be a place where there is an expectation of hearing how and why people decided to follow Jesus. You want also to have a culture where people talk about what God is doing in their lives right now. Once you have developed this 'culture' you will find it much easier for the young people in the group to feel sufficiently comfortable to speak to the group.

'Same time next week!'

If you feel that the group is a bit nervous about giving testimonies, tell them what you are hoping to do, but not this week. Explain that the leaders have given their testimony and 'now it's **your** turn'. Tell the group there will be an opportunity for anyone who is keen to talk about following Jesus the following week. This will give young people in the group time to think it over.

Practise in small groups

It can be very helpful to have some of the young people give their testimony in their small group (either in their weekly Bible study or discussion group). This can be a great way to prepare them and ease the way.

One last thing

When you hear a testimony that is moving, it may be appropriate to enjoy what has just happened and not to ask for another.

Four ways of giving testimonies or testifying

The Classic

The leader explains what a testimony is and asks for volunteers to come forward and testify.

The Interview

An interview is one of the simplest ways to have a testimony time. The leader interviews the person giving his or her testimony. A variation of this would be to have a young person interview another young person (maybe a good friend).

Living Legends!

Invite elderly members of your congregation to come to youth group and give their testimony. You may find that the kids will be blown away to hear from someone who became a Christian in the 1940s! This can benefit your youth group and the church generally. The young people will see that not all Christians are teenagers or in their early twenties. And the older members of the congregation will no doubt be encouraged to see young people who are seeking to follow Jesus. Not only will they be encouraged, they will probably begin to pray for the group. (There may also be the added benefit of developing cross-generational relationships between the young and the old. Too often, the youth group is seen as an extended wing of the church with no real connection to other members.)

Testify!

This is different to telling how you became a Christian. Instead of asking for a testimony, you ask for people to talk about what God is doing in their lives at present or what he has done recently. One youth group runs a segment called 'Jesus @ Work'. This is a time for the people in the group to share what Jesus is doing in their lives. It has been very successful. This may take some time to succeed in your group but stay with it. It is worth the effort.

How to run a testimony time

Step 1: Decide who is going to run it.

Step 2: Choose how you are going to run it.

Step 3: Explain to the group what you are asking for (either a testimony or a time to testify). Explain also how you are going to do it.

Step 4: Ask for a volunteer.

Step 5: When he or she finishes, ask someone in the group to pray for the volunteer.

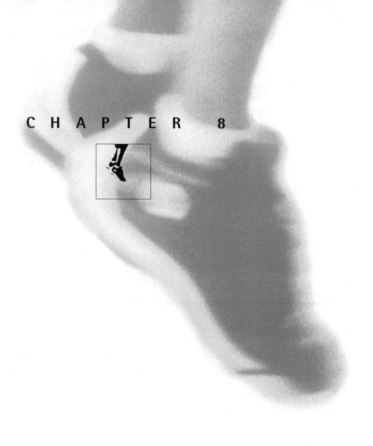

CHAPTER 8

BRW (Bible reading of the week)

Key thought:	A time where various individuals encourage the group by talking about what they are reading and learning from God's word.
Reflection:	Are the young people actively encouraged to read their Bibles during the week? If so, is there an opportunity to share with each other what they have learned or been challenged by? Are they 'spurred on to love and good deeds' as they hear from each other week by week?

What then shall we say, brothers? When you come together, everyone has a hymn, or a word of instruction, a revelation, a tongue or an interpretation. All of these must be done for the strengthening of the church (1 Corinthians 14:26).

Therefore encourage one another and build each other up, just as in fact you are doing (1 Thessalonians 5:11).

All Scripture is God-breathed and is useful for teaching, rebuking, correcting and training in righteousness (2 Timothy 3:16).

A helpful component to a youth group meeting is a time of sharing what the members of the group have learned from the Bible. We call it 'BRW' or Bible Reading of the Week. A leader (or competent young person) stands up in front of the group and says, 'We are now going to have a BRW. That is, a time to share with the group what you have been reading in the Bible this week. It can be a verse that challenged you or something that encouraged you and you would like to tell us about it.' The person leading the BRW then waits for people to take up the offer and come to the front (or stand up where they are) and share. This can be a great addition as it encourages the group to read God's word and be prepared to talk about it with others.

Some helpful hints

This segment may take more effort to introduce successfully to the meeting. It is one of those things that requires 'guts'. Do not spring this on the group without adequate preparation.

Effective ways to introduce BRWs

Begin BRWs at a weekend or overnight camp. As part of the morning programme, send out the group to have personal devotions (we call them 'quiet times'). Give each member of the group a sheet of paper with an encouragement to pray and a suggested Bible passage to read. (We include this in the camp booklets we give each camper.) It also includes a few questions to help provoke thought on the passage. After an appropriate time (20 to 30 minutes), call the group together and spend some time talking together about what they have just read. If the group is functioning well, that is, there is a level of trust and comfort among most of the people involved, then you may find that the young people will be open to talking about what they have just read. When you include BRW in your weekly meeting you will have something to refer to. You can say, 'This is the same as we did on the camp'.

Give out weekly Devotion/Quiet Time sheets

Encourage the young people in your group to spend time reading the Bible during the week. One effective way to do this is each week at the youth gathering hand out a sheet of paper for weekly devotions or quiet times. You might just find that many of the young people in your group use them! This will give you a platform to launch from the following week. For example, if you give them a sheet of paper with four simple devotions on the book of James you can then ask, 'Who had a look at the book of James this week? Okay, we are now going to give anyone a chance to share with the group what encouraged or challenged you from this book. Who wants to give it a shot?' You may find that they will take up this opportunity.

The leaders begin

The leaders can get the ball rolling with the BRW. You can spend a number of weeks having the various leaders (or 'special guests' if you are leading solo) come to the front and talk about what they have been reading the previous week. This will help to bring about a 'culture of sharing' and may make it much easier for the young people to take up the challenge.

Introduce BRW in small groups

Finally, small groups may be the time and place to include this component in your programme. Young people often feel safe in their small groups. If you think that your group may not be ready, introduce BRWs in the small groups.

Two helpful ideas

BRW Impromptu dramas

One helpful and fun way to share what you have learned from God's word is for volunteers to work out a skit or short drama to present to the group what they have read the previous week. If there are a number of volunteers you can form the whole group into smaller groups and have a number of skits. If there are only one or two volunteers you can send them out to prepare during Spotlight or a Bible game and present their BRW skit after the segment is over.

Pray after BRW

If a number of kids talk about things they have read during the week, or if even one person shares, it may be helpful to pray for them afterwards. Spend some time thanking God for what he has shown them that week.

Example

The first time we ran BRW it didn't go that well. The kids in the group were unprepared and we sprang it on them without warning. No one spoke. We were undaunted. The next week we tried again. The person leading the BRW explained what we were doing, gave an example and then asked for any volunteers. After a moment of silence a girl in our group put her hand in the air and came forward. This girl was very shy and had hardly uttered a word all year. Suddenly the group became silent and there was an air of expectancy. The girl went to the front of the group and without looking at anyone, read out 2 Timothy 1:7, 'For God did not give us a spirit of timidity, but a spirit of power, of love and of self discipline.' She then said, 'All my life I have been shy. Please pray that I won't be so timid.' She sat down without looking at anyone. You could have cut the air with a knife. The leader wisely did not ask for any more volunteers and prayed for what we had just heard. It was one of those moments where you knew God was at work and something big had just happened. BRW was never the same after that. She had shown us what God's word could do. (By the way, she is no longer as timid. She is a leader in our youth group and a student at Bible college.)

How to run a BRW

Step 1: Choose who is going to run a time of sharing from the Bible.

Step 2: Decide how you are going to run it.

Step 3: The person running it explains what will happen, asks for volunteers and runs the segment.

Step 4. Pray about what has been shared.

CHAPTER 9

Operation World

Key thought:	It can be very helpful to find out about another country or culture in order to pray for it.
Reflection:	Is your group praying for the spread of the gospel throughout the world? Do the young people realise that there are countries where it is very difficult to be a Christian? Is the group aware that many people in this world experience constant war and/or poverty? Do they know that in some countries very few people are committed to Jesus?

Operation World by Patrick Johnston has had a great impact on many Christians throughout the world. This book lists every country in the world and provides helpful statistics and prayer points. Use the book to facilitate better prayer in your youth group. It will be helpful for young people to hear about another country that is different and maybe less fortunate than their own. They can then pray for that country.

How to run Operation World

You need to buy the book or the latest version of *Operation World* on CDRom (this can be purchased from most Christian booksellers or on the internet www.gmi.org/ow). Either a leader, or better, a young person in the group, prepares to lead Operation World (OW) once or twice a month. They choose a country and present a brief (under two minute) report on it. The group then prays specifically for that country or it can lead into your regular prayer time. OW is a great way to shift the focus of your group onto the bigger picture. It can also be a way to pray for a country that is in the news (such as Israel or Iraq).

Further Ideas

Operation World Night

Have a night that focuses on praying for other countries. Set up three or four corners of the room as different countries (you can make up a poster with the name of the country, in the area representing the country put out some pictures, artefacts etc.). Using the book *Operation World*, make up information sheets about each country, giving facts as well as prayer points. Gather everyone together and tell them that today youth group will be different. Announce that you are sending them to other countries (a trip around the world). Just for fun explain to them that they will be flying and give them a packet of chips and a drink to make the trip more comfortable. You could even have someone give a run down of what happens before the plane takes off and play a tape of a plane taking off. (Note: the trip is only short.) Once you have taken them into the hall you can keep them together as a large group or break them into smaller groups. They go to one area and learn about a country (from the information sheets you have prepared) and pray for it. You may like to have someone dressed as a local to talk about the country. They then move on to the next country. Keep going until all groups have visited each country. You can finish by taking them back to the plane and flying them home to their own suburb. You can then lead a study related to mission, evangelism, prayer or the like.

Operation World Social Night

You could hold a social based around OW. The group could eat at a number of different restaurants related to a certain country. Each time you do this you could have a brief look at the facts and figures about that country. If you were brave you could have a brief prayer time in the restaurant. For example, you could start at one restaurant, then move to another for the main course. You could then move on and have dessert consisting of ice cream or gelato.[1] This would make for a memorable (and tasty) night. If you don't want to go out, hold it at your church (or in someone's home). There can be food from various

---

1.   Gelato would obviously be Italy. Many ice cream places have names related to a country such as Danish or New Zealand ice cream. You could also have a starter like French fries or some other snack that relates to a particular country.

countries and you can present an OW at various stages throughout the night. You could then pray for each country.

Jesus Freak

This is a variation of OW. Instead of looking at a country and then praying for it, spend a couple of minutes reflecting on people who have suffered or are presently suffering for the Christian faith. To do this, get a copy of the book *Jesus Freak* by DC Talk and the Voice of the Martyrs (Albury Publishing, Tulsa Oklahoma. 1999). This book tells the stories of people, young and old who have suffered and even died for following Jesus. Give the book to a young person for a week or so and ask them to find a chapter or section that they find encouraging or moving. They can either report on the chapter or read it out to the group at the next youth meeting. You can then pray for the people or that country. You could also link it to an Operation World. This will really open the eyes of some of the young people in your group as to what some Christians have suffered because they follow Jesus.

How to run Operation World

Step 1: Choose a person to run OW. It may be helpful if this person runs it regularly or for a certain period of time (say six months or a year).

Step 2: Choose a country, and read the relevant section in *Operation World.*

Step 3: Present a report on the country. It could be helpful to have a map showing the location of the country.

Step 4: Pray for the country or, follow OW with prayer time and the country becomes the first prayer point.

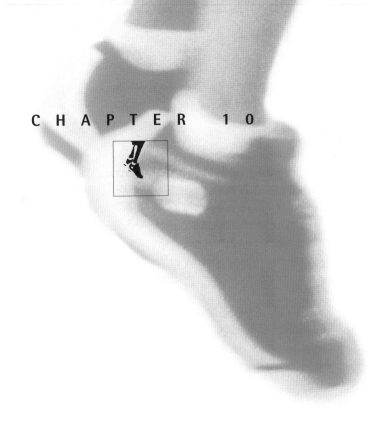

C H A P T E R   1 0

Predicament!

Key thought:	Prepare your group for godly responses to real situations.
Reflection:	We need Christian young people who are prepared to change the world for Christ in all situations. Are the young people in your group prepared to make a wise choice when faced with difficult decisions? Can they make godly decisions when confronted with a tricky situation?

Be self-controlled and alert. Your enemy the devil prowls around like a roaring lion looking for someone to devour. (1 Peter 5:8)

Predicament is a great way to add fun and relevant Bible teaching to your group[1]. It is also very easy to do. Set up a situation that young people are likely to encounter. The predicament is to reflect a real scenario where they must make a choice. The group

---

1.   The idea for Predicament came from *The Youth Worker's Guide to Creative Bible Study* by Karen Dockrey, Victor Books, 1991.

discusses the situation and offers various solutions. You then provide them with wisdom and answers from the Bible on the topic.

Example

A good 'predicament' to begin with could be the pressure to drink alcohol or get drunk at a party. Begin by quickly explaining to the group that, 'Most of us, at one time or another, will be invited to a party. Parties can be great times of fun and friendship. However, you can often find yourself under pressure to do things that you shouldn't. For instance, some of your friends may try to get you to drink alcohol... Instead of me standing up here and explaining the situation, let's act it out.' You then ask a number of volunteers to come up and act it out. These volunteers 'illustrate the predicament'. To act out the scene you need only two or three people. One or two people encourage the other to get drunk. Their job is nothing more than to set up the predicament. They do not provide any answers. After acting out the predicament, the youth group discusses possible solutions in pairs or small groups. After a few minutes the leader asks for volunteers to say how they would deal with this predicament. They can even come to the front and act it out! This can then lead to a giant group discussion and/or a leader giving a talk and providing some helpful answers.

(While you need only a few people, it can be a case of 'the more the merrier'. When we did this Predicament we had a whole host of characters. We had dancers, people mingling to create a crowd, a disc jockey, we even had a young man acting like a lamppost! It was his idea. If there aren't enough people in your group for this, just have the main characters.)

HOT TIP We have found it helpful occasionally to run our whole youth meeting around a predicament. For example, 'What do you do when you have an enemy?' We began with a situation, 'Devise an enemy. It must be truly nasty and evil.' The kids talked this over with the person next to them. We then asked for volunteers to draw a picture of the enemy on the white board showing this to the rest of the group. This was great fun as we had all sorts of crazy drawings (most were of the variety you would see in a Spiderman comic). We also learned a memory verse related to this (Luke 6:27 'Love your enemies.'). Then came the predicament. We asked the kids to form groups and act out a real life predicament they had faced that dealt with an enemy or someone who strongly disliked them. We then did a study on Luke 6:27–36 (love your enemies ... turn the other cheek) and had a discussion and teaching time about loving our enemies. We finished with a prayer time revolving around loving and forgiving our enemies. It was a very helpful, fun meeting.

There are a wide variety of topics that can be a predicament. Here are some that we have explored:

You are tempted to go out with someone who is not a follower of Jesus.
You have a fight with friends.
You have to forgive someone for a wrong they have done to you.
Someone puts pressure on you to do things sexually.
Someone puts pressure on you to drink alcohol.

(These topics along with the relevant Bible verses are in the Resources section on page 130.)

Helpful hints

Pick relevant topics

Choose predicaments that are relevant to your group (or will be in the near future). Your goal is to help prepare your group for real life situations they will face. You want them to have the tools to make wise, God honouring decisions.

Prepare handouts

It can be very helpful to prepare a paper with relevant Bible verses to hand out when you give the talk or have a discussion. Helpful Bible references are given on pages 130–133.

Ask the young people to prepare a predicament

A great way to run Predicament is for some of the young people in the group to do it. They can either run the whole thing, including giving Bible verses and answers at the end, or they can set the scene and a leader can take care of the rest.

Example

We asked a young man in our group to run predicament. A week later he was ready. The situation he came up with was, 'What do you do when there is a fight on the train?' He takes the train home every day from school and had witnessed a fight earlier that week. While I would have never come up with this idea, it was very real to him and others in the group. It led to a helpful discussion and a solid time searching the Bible for answers.

Don't overdo it

Predicaments work well in short series. Do it for three or four weeks in a row a couple of times a year.

Final words

We have found Predicament to be a great addition to our youth ministry. It is vibrant, fun and centred around relevant teaching from the Bible that will have an immediate impact in the lives of the young people in the group.

How to run Predicament

Step 1: Introduce the subject to the group.

Step 2: Ask for volunteers to come forward and 'set the scene' in an impromptu drama.

Step 3: Ask the young people to discuss with those around them what they would do in the predicament presented to them.

Step 4: Ask for volunteers to give some advice as to what they think Christians should do when faced with the particular predicament. They can either shout out an answer when called upon or, gather some friends together to come to the front of the group and act out what they would do in the predicament. Spend plenty of time on their suggestions as this allows for a variety of solutions and also reveals the different views held by members of the youth group.

Step 5: Give a handout with Bible verses that address the particular situation.

Step 6: Ask for volunteers one by one to read through each verse and then comment on the verse or allow comments from the group. This can lead to a group discussion or a talk by the leader on the subject.

Step 7: Have a time of prayer about what you have just discussed. Pray that each member of the group will have strength and wisdom the next time they face a similar predicament.

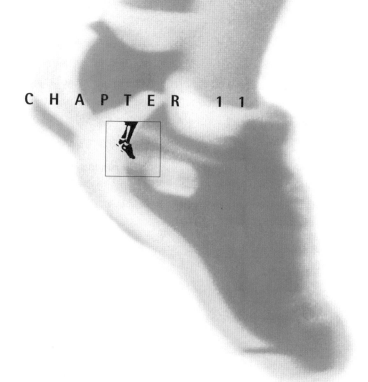

CHAPTER 11

Scalpel

Key thought:	Critique or dissect an aspect of modern culture from a biblical perspective.[1]
Reflection:	Are the kids in your group being taught to examine their world from a Christian perspective? Are they equipped to deal with the pressures put on them by the media? Can they respond in a godly way to things like unhelpful magazines or music video clips?

'The eye is the lamp of the body. If your eyes are good, your whole body will be full of light. But if your eyes are bad, your whole body will be full of darkness. If then the light within you is darkness, how great is that darkness!' (Matthew. 6:22,23)

Scalpel is a time to reflect on some aspect of modern culture from a Christian perspective. You can choose music, advertising, or a television show. You won't have to look much further than a popular music video. Whoever is doing the dissection (you could call

---

1. Thanks to Jodie McNeil for this idea.

them the surgeon or the doctor) presents the item for critique. (For well-known songs or advertisements they may need only remind the group rather than actually show it.) After presenting or reminding the group of the item, they point out the unhelpful aspects of its message. They would present some wisdom from the Bible and offer some help as to the godly and wise way to live.

One leader, who runs a similar segment, briefly examines a song or popular advertisement and asks four questions: What is this person trying to say? Why are they saying this? What does God say in response (a look at the Bible)? What must our response be?[2]

Scalpel is best done in a short series (two or three in a row, twice or three times a year) or it can be linked to a teaching series. It would also be a good segment for a young person in the group to run.

Scalpel is a great way not only to critique our culture, but also teach the Bible in a relevant and refreshing way.

How to run Scalpel

Step 1: Choose who will run the segment.

Step2: The person chooses an item to dissect/critique.

Step 3: Present the item.

Step 4: Seek to understand what the thinking is behind the item on show.

Step 5: Point out the dangers in the item and briefly present a biblical view.

Step 6: Have a group discussion (if appropriate).

---

2.   Dave Esdale from Glenbrook Anglican Church suggested this approach.

C H A P T E R   1 2

Flag

Key thought:	A segment where individuals tell the group about occasions when they have 'flown a flag' for Jesus by showing others they were Christians. Whether bold or subtle, Flag is telling someone that our relationship with Jesus makes a difference to our lives.
Reflection:	Are the young people in your group trying to reflect to others the difference Christ has made in their lives? Are they seeking to 'take every opportunity' to show those around them what it means to be a Christian?

Be wise in the way you act toward outsiders; make the most of every opportunity.
(Colossians 4:5)

Witnessing for Jesus takes different forms. It can be bold and clear cut—telling someone about Jesus and his death on the cross. It can be subtle – telling a person you work with that you go to church and why. Flag is an opportunity for young people (and leaders) to tell the group about times when they showed they were Christian and gave some sort of witness for Christ.

How Flag began

At a weekend away with my youth group the speaker talked about 'flying a flag for Jesus'. He told us to take every opportunity to show those around us that we are Christians. When we came home, my wife suggested we introduce a segment called 'Flag' in youth group and in church. Members of the group are encouraged to talk about something they have done the previous week that has shown their neighbours, classmates, workmates or family that they are different because they follow Jesus. It has been a great encouragement to hear about a young man who reads his Bible in between pizza deliveries at work, or the girl who has a Bible verse glued to her school workbook.

Example

The father of one of the girls in our group was looking for a job. She told the group and we prayed for her and for her dad. When she went home after church that night she decided to tell her dad that we had prayed for him. He was not a Christian so this was a fairly gutsy move. She hoped that this would be a small flag to show him that she was a Christian and that she cared for him. In her words, 'He just chuckled to himself.' The next day he found a job. A day or so later he thanked her and told her that her prayers had meant a great deal to him. What a great flag for Christ.

How to run Flag

A leader comes to the front, explains what will happen in Flag, and asks for volunteers. To begin, it could be helpful to have a Bible study series on being bold for Jesus or on evangelism. One group has made an actual flag to put up during the segment. When we lead Flag, we often give a brief outline of what various flags stand for (a white flag = surrender; a skull and crossbones = pirates). We then talk about raising a flag for Christ.

Variations

A variation to the standard Flag is 'Love Flag' when the group talks about times they have been able to show love to someone or do a loving thing.

How to run Flag

Step 1: Choose who will run this segment.

Step 2: This person explains Flag to the group and why it is important to witness for Christ.

Step 3: Ask for volunteers to share times when they 'flew a flag'.

Step 4: If appropriate, pray for the person witnessed to.

C H A P T E R 1 3

Favourite tunes

Key thought:	It can be encouraging for the group when someone plays a Christian song that they have found meaningful.
Reflection:	Are the young people in your group enjoying some of the great Christian music that is on offer?

Music is a powerful force in the lives of young people. It shapes the clothes they wear, the way they speak and sometimes even the way they think. Therefore, it is helpful to provide young people with music that is not only of great quality but also helpful to their Christian life. There is an amazing amount of good Christian music available to listen to. Include a segment in the programme where the kids bring in a Christian song that is meaningful to them. They play their favourite song for the group (with the lyrics on an overhead or printed out) and explain why they like the song. With a bit of prior notice, you could link the songs with the topic or section of the Bible you are studying in the meeting. You may find this becomes a significant time as the young people tell the rest of group something meaningful about themselves. The leaders may need to do this for a few weeks to get things started (provided they listen to good Christian music and don't try to sneak in some Pavarotti).

Include a music segment from time to time, maybe once a month. Or, you could run it for a few weeks in a row a couple of times a year.

How to run Favourite Tune

Step 1: Someone is asked or volunteers to present a song he or she likes.

Step 2: This person prints/writes up the lyrics for all to see (before the meeting).

Step 3: The person leading gives a brief explanation of why he or she likes the song or how it has helped.

Step 4: Play the song.

HOT TIP you may want to show the music video to the song if you are able. This may make it more interesting and relevant.

CHAPTER 14

Running effective prayer times

Key thought:	A Christian youth group must be characterised by prayer. Make prayer a regular and exciting part of your weekly time together.
Reflection:	Prayer is a fundamental element in the life of a Christian. Is your youth group characterised by regular prayer? Are the young people being taught and encouraged to pray regularly? Is prayer modelled each week in youth group? If it is a struggle to have a prayer time in your youth group why is this so? Are there any changes you can make to overcome this?

Devote yourselves to prayer, being watchful and thankful. (Colossians 4:2)

... pray continually; (1 Thessalonians 5:17)

But you, dear friends, build yourselves up in your most holy faith and pray in the Holy Spirit. (Jude 1:20)

When I think of the Christian life I think of Jesus, reading the Scriptures, meeting with other Christians, and praying. In fact, there are few things more fundamentally Christian than prayer. We have a God who longs to hear our prayers and promises to answer them. As soon as I became a Christian I became a person who prayed. Yet, while Christians are to be people who pray, our youth groups are often quite the opposite. I would go so far as to say that it is rare to find a youth group that is characterised by regular, consistent and healthy prayer.

Why is this so? I'm fairly certain I don't need to convince you of the power of prayer. Similarly, I probably don't need to convince you of the fact that the Bible encourages us to be people committed to prayer. (See Ephesians 6:18, Colossians 4:2, 1 Thessalonians 5:17. If you need more convincing, spend a few hours looking up the word 'pray' with a concordance.) If this is true, prayer must be part of our weekly programmes. Sadly, I have found that this just isn't the case. In fact, I have found that many groups don't even begin their weekly programmes with a simple request for God to bless the time together. Following on from this, many groups wouldn't consider having a time devoted to group prayer and give reasons like:

'We're trying to reach nonChristians. We don't want to alienate the newcomers.'
'The kids in the group wouldn't cope with a time of prayer. They are too rowdy!'

This is a disaster. How can we show God to people by hiding our dependence on him? One of the best ways to reach out to those who don't know Christ is to show them that there is a spiritual reality undergirding this world. In other words, we must demonstrate that we are people who depend on our heavenly Father to help us along. We must show them that he can help them as well. We may feel that prayer is unattractive, when in reality it is a fantastic way to witness to this dying world. Furthermore, we are neglecting the spiritual growth of the Christian kids in our groups by not encouraging them to pray regularly. If you are not running regular prayer times, change things this week!

Example

Some time ago I led a two-week training course on youth ministry. When we were discussing the weekly meeting I told the group to make sure they opened in prayer. In my naiveté, I just assumed that everyone did this so I didn't spend more than a minute on it. Weeks later I met with a youth leader who told me that this little fact had made a large impact on his group. Previously they didn't pray at the start. When they began with prayer, it helped to show everyone present that this was a time where they would focus on God and following Jesus. While it is exciting that they have discovered this, why did it take so long? Why didn't previous leaders implement this obvious and simple step?

Six Key Thoughts on Running a Prayer Time

1. Prayer reflects our dependence on God

A youth group that does not pray regularly is a poor reflection of a Christian youth group. That sounds a bit extreme I know, but spend a moment or two and think about what makes up a Christian group. Bible study, holiness, and prayer must be central to our practice. For too long, we have been satisfied running 'prayerless' groups built on hollow excuses (we are seeking to reach nonChristians, we don't want to shock our kids). If you pray 'every now and then' or do not have regular corporate prayer times, you are running a group that does not reflect its dependence on God. This must change immediately.

2. Teach your group the necessity of prayer

You have no doubt noticed that I am assuming the kids in your group will cope when it comes to prayer. If you have been reading this and saying, 'Yeah right, you don't know my group. Getting them to pray like this will be about as easy as getting them to place their hands on a hot frying pan!' May I suggest that you spend a few months correcting the sins of the past. Begin by teaching your group the necessity of prayer. Lead the group into a healthy prayer life by modelling what it means to be a mature follower of Jesus. Seek to equip the Christian kids in the group so that they can pray effectively. This will take some time and may not come easily but it is of the utmost importance that you begin right away.

3. Prayer is an integral component of a healthy group

If some kids leave because you have initiated a prayer time, you must proceed anyway. When some groups have decided to bring in more Christian content (like healthy prayer times) this may lead to a decline in numbers. The kids make excuses like 'the group isn't fun anymore'. Instead of desperately changing the programmeme to bring them back, you must press ahead with nonnegotiable elements like prayer. Your group must be dedicated to building strong Christians. These strong young people can then reach out to their friends. It may be painful, but if some kids leave over an issue like group prayer, you would have lost them in the long run anyway.

4. The leaders must lead

Prayer is a key part of your programme where the leaders must set the tone and help the young people in the group. Leaders are there to help draw the members of the group into a closer relationship with Jesus. Therefore, the leaders must be totally supportive of the need and necessity for prayer.

5. Silence is OK

One trap that many leaders fall into is trying to 'rescue' a prayer time if there is a long period of silence. This is unhelpful. It teaches the kids in the group that ultimately they don't need to pray. The leaders will do it for them. It is fine for there to be some silence during prayer times, especially when the group is just starting out. If there is silence, we tell the kids in our group, 'That's no problem. Just pray silently and I will close at an appropriate time.' The kids will cope. (By the way, the leaders mustn't 'rescue' rule goes for any component of your programme that requires group participation. Never let the kids think that if they don't volunteer or participate, the leaders will cover it.)

6. Pray for your prayers

If your group isn't a mass of prayer warriors just yet, pray that they will become better prayers. Spend time in your leaders' meetings, at church, privately and in the youth group itself praying for a better prayer life within the group. This is one prayer that God will love to answer!

If your group isn't used to praying (or it is a real struggle)

Teach them

Spend time regularly showing the young people the how and why to have an effective prayer life. Your leaders (or you) must do this every chance you have. Invite leaders, parents or elders to visit and give a short testimony on how God has worked in their life through prayer. Give a series of Bible studies on the subject. Or, before each prayer time, give a brief Bible study on a relevant text or passage. (See *Changing the World*, p64.) On each occasion show the group the relevance and importance of prayer.

Model it

The best way to teach young people to pray is to have leaders model prayer to those in their small group (assuming you are running small groups). One of the 'golden rules' of youth ministry is that young people will imitate their leaders (see *Changing the World*, p29). If a godly leader regularly runs a prayer time in a small group, it will not be long before some of the young people in the group begin to pray as well. We must constantly model prayer. Institute times of spontaneous prayer. If someone tells you something that you know you could pray for, do it on the spot. Say to the young person, 'We should pray for that.' Then go ahead and pray a short prayer. That will demonstrate to the group member that prayer is important.

Be Patient

For most groups, good prayer times will not happen overnight. You may be taking a group of young people to a place they have rarely visited (the land of prayer). Stay with it—with God's help you'll get there.

How to lead a prayer time

A good prayer time needs someone to lead it. It is fairly simple, but it may take some practice.

Understand what you are trying to do

Leaders must understand what they hope to accomplish. You are not having a prayer time because it is 'good for you'. Nor are you praying because if you don't 'God will be angry'. You are having a prayer time because you have a relationship with your heavenly Father and you rely on him for help and strength. You also desire, as a group, to praise him and you wish to support each other in prayer.

Plan how you will lead

There are many ways to run group prayer. Leaders must have a clear idea of what they plan to do. The way we usually do it is to draw two columns on a whiteboard or overhead, one with the heading 'thanks' (or praise) and the other 'ask' (or help). The leader then writes down various points from the group. Once the board has a good number of things to pray for, the leader tells the group he/she will start the prayer time and ask someone in the group who will be comfortable about it to finish with a closing prayer when the time is right. (More ways to pray are suggested later in this chapter.)

Be encouraging and, if necessary, explain the importance of prayer

It is a good thing to regularly remind the group why it is so important to pray. Use an appropriate Bible verse or go through the Lord's Prayer. Leaders could give a brief testimony on how their prayers have been answered. Or you could begin with a short testimony by one of the young people in the group. It may also be necessary to encourage the group not to be shy or embarrassed about praying aloud.

Be creative with your prayer times

While we must never make prayer a gimmick, it can be helpful to be creative. Spend time thinking through effective ways to pray as a group.

Example

One of my goals in ministry is to train leaders by setting them an example to follow. They then set an example for the kids in the group to follow. Prayer time is a classic example of this. My wife and I led prayer times for a while and then gave it to some of the leaders to run. Soon the kids themselves were keen to take over adding their own brand of creativity. One Sunday afternoon before youth group started, I asked a young man we call P.C. if he could run a prayer time. 'No problem,' he said. Later that afternoon during the youth group meeting he ran a prayer time based around a spreadsheet. He turned to the whiteboard and divided it into four columns. At the top of the first column was: Whose prayer point it was; the second column indicated whether it was thanks or a request; the third noted what the prayer point was; and the fourth heading was who was going to pray for it. I would have never thought of this. To a computer crazy fourteen year old young man, it was quite natural, and in my opinion, quite brilliant.

What if no one prays?

No problem. Encourage the group week by week that God hears their prayers whether spoken or silent. Do not rush things just because you feel that no one will pray. The group needs to learn that this is important and will be a consistent part of the programme. Make sure that you and the other leaders are relaxed. Never scold the group and remember, leaders must never rescue the prayer time. Silence is quite okay. After a short time conclude with a closing prayer and move on to the next part of your programme. If you and the other leaders are comfortable with silence, the chances are that the group will become comfortable with it as well. Eventually, the silence will be slowly filled with prayers spoken out loud.

Final thoughts

- Prayer doesn't need to be jazzed up too much. It isn't meant to be flashy, it is meant to be a regular part of your programme. Therefore, don't worry if you can't come up with too many fancy ways to pray. In my youth group, we spend most weeks simply doing the 'ask/help' model. The kids in the group realise that part of coming to youth group is to pray for each other. This has taken pressure off the leaders to make prayer extra snazzy each week.

- It may be helpful to keep a record of what you have prayed for. It is amazing to see how many of your prayers have been answered. This will encourage the group to stay with it.

- We have found it helpful to form a 'prayer team'. This is a group of volunteers who will organise prayer meetings and list prayer points for the non-youth members of our congregation to receive. This has led to our holding regular youth prayer nights. Run by the team, these are excellent nights of concentrated prayer.

HOT TIP Run a 'Prayer Night'

Have some of the young people in your group organise a night of prayer. This is a time where anyone from the youth group and the church can come together to pray. We do this a couple of times a year. We break it into four segments: a time of confession, a time to pray for the world, a time to pray for our country, and finally, a time to pray for personal prayer points and needs related to our church/youth group. The first three are done as a big group, the last is done in small groups. This has always been great night of encouragement for the group.

12 great ways to pray

1. Pray short prayers

If your group is not used to praying, begin by suggesting that they pray short, one sentence prayers. You can have a time of 'thanks' where you encourage kids to say simple things like, 'Thanks for my parents.' Or, 'Thanks for friends.' These prayers are simple and straightforward. This can lead to longer prayers later on.

2. Thanks/Help

On a sheet of paper/overhead/whiteboard draw two columns; one column headed 'thanks' and the other 'help'. Whoever is running the prayer time (either a leader or an able Christian young person) takes requests from the group and then you proceed to pray for the points on the board. You can soon add a third column, 'APs' or answered prayers. The leader can mention the previous prayer requests, which have since been answered. This is a great encouragement to the group and a real witness to those who aren't Christians.

3. The world/(your country)/us

This is similar to the previous idea. Make three columns on your whiteboard or overhead transparency. These columns represent three different areas to pray for: the needs of this world, the needs of your country and personal requests. Variations on this theme are: 'Global/national/local' or 'a long way away/ closer/ real close'. Same deal, yet with a different flavour.

4. Concentric circles

Draw a series of circles within each other like a dartboard. The outer circle is the world, the next circle is your country, the next is your city, then personal requests. In each circle you can write in appropriate prayer points. The leader leads the group and tells them when to move to the next circle.

5. P.R.A.Y. (not yarp!)

I know of a group that encourages the kids to 'P.R.A.Y. not yarp'. They break the word 'pray' into an anagram P= praise, R= repent, A= ask and Y= yourself (personal requests). They tell the young people in their group they must do things in the correct order and not 'yarp' (yourself, ask, repent, praise). I think this is clever and helpful for the group.
(Thanks to Northmead Anglican Church for this idea.)

6. Small groups

Form into small groups and spend some time praying. The whole group can share prayer points and then pray in small groups, or they can share requests in the groups themselves. A variation of this is to break the group into pairs/triplets and give each pair/triplet one point to pray for. The leader then closes the prayer time when appropriate.

7. Pray Scripture

It is helpful to use a Bible verse to help you pray. For instance, if there were some members of the group going through a stressful time, write 1 Peter 5:7–11 on the whiteboard/overhead or projector slide (or read it aloud). You could then pray for things that are causing anxiety. You could do this with Philippians 4:6, Luke 12:22–34 or the Lord's Prayer.

8. Pray for each other

It can be helpful for members of the group to write down things they need prayer for in the coming week. Collect each piece of paper and then hand them out randomly. This provides the group with some things to pray for. It also promotes unity and a sense of caring for each other outside the weekly gathering.

9. Allocate prayer points

If your group is up to it, ask for volunteers to pray for the various prayer points. This means that the prayer time won't fall flat and that all prayer requests are covered. It also means that one person won't pray for all the prayer points. (When asking for volunteers don't put anyone on the spot unless you are sure they will cope.)

10. Reflection

We have found it helpful to have a time where the group sits silently and quietly prays. The person leading will read out some Scriptures, maybe a Psalm or a passage about Jesus. The group will reflect on this and pray silently. The leader can also suggest some topics to pray for (world peace, reaching out to the local community). We have found this to be a helpful addition to our programme.

11. Solitary prayer

After sharing prayer points, send the group out for a time of solitary prayer. After an appropriate time, between 5 and15 minutes, ring a bell, blow a whistle, shout, bang two pots together – whatever it takes to get them back together. To do this effectively, there must a high degree of trust that the kids actually will go and pray.

12. Pray around the circle for the person next to you

The group sits in a circle. After a time of sharing prayer points the group prays for each other. They do this by praying clockwise in a circle one person after the other. If someone feels uncomfortable praying aloud they merely tap the next person along and this person prays instead. (This style of prayer is only for those groups that are comfortable with each other and with praying aloud.)

How to run a prayer time

Step 1: Choose who will run the prayer time.

Step 2: Decide how it will be run.

Step 3: Explain to the group how you will pray this week.

Step 4: Take prayer points.

Step 5: Pray.

CHAPTER 15

Singing

Here is a brief outline from the Bible as to why singing is an important part of the Christian gathering.

Why do we sing?

Psalm 96 and 100; Jeremiah 30:19

Singing is a way of expressing our worship of God. We sing to praise his name and his deeds.

Acts 16:25

Paul and Silas sang praises to God despite their surroundings (they were in jail). This was also a witness to other prisoners and guards.

Ephesians 5:18–21; Sing psalms, hymns and spiritual songs

We sing because it is a characteristic of people who are filled with the Holy Spirit. It is an appropriate way to express thanks to God.

Colossians 3:16

As we sing the words of Christ can dwell in us richly. It can be a method for teaching Christ's word. Singing is also a way of expressing gratitude to God.

James 5:13

If you're happy sing songs of praise to God.

(Singing gone wrong)

Ezekiel 26:13 and 33:32

Graham Thomas is a youth leader whom I have known for over 10 years. When he was a young man he bought a guitar, took some lessons and was soon leading the youth band at our church. He is experienced in helping churches develop singing in their youth programmes. At the beginning of this year, he joined a youth group with around 20 young people. The group never sang in their weekly gathering, but he soon changed that. The group now sings regularly. I asked him to share some of his thoughts on developing singing in the weekly youth meeting.

How do you bring singing into a youth group from nothing?

In today's culture many young people grow up singing only the national anthem and a few pop songs in the shower. You may need to think strategically about how you can warm the hearts of the kids so they will want to have singing in the programme. Corporate singing at youth group may not be a natural thing for them to do. It may be necessary to give them a positive experience of singing to convince them that it can be worthwhile. This could be done at a combined youth night or a camp with another church. You could also have a musician from another church come and visit your group. I know of one youth leader who introduced singing into a youth group by having a singer come and sing to the group. She sang a few songs and then asked if the group would join in for a couple of songs. It worked well.

You could also have a teaching series on 'great songs of the Bible'. (You could examine some of the Psalms, Exodus 15, Revelation 4:8–11). Find some well-known Christian songs that are taken from Scripture. After the talk/study on this song (why they were singing, what they said about God), you could learn the song and sing it together. An example of this is Lamentations 3:22,23. This is a great part of the Bible and there is a chorus that comes directly from it. This could help get the group fired up to sing.

Finding and training a musician/song leader

While you are preparing your group to sing, look for someone in the group (leader or young person) who can lead the singing. This means they will probably have to learn an instrument – acoustic guitar is by far the best choice because it doesn't take too long to reach a standard where people can sing along with you. Furthermore, it is portable and rhythmic.

It may be easier to find a musician than you think. Someone may be learning an instrument on the quiet, so to speak. Find that person and encourage them, not necessarily to play in front of the group straight away, but perhaps just to keep playing. Many young people stop learning an instrument because they are not encouraged to keep playing, or, they have no reason to play it (other than their parents forcing them!).

In my experience it takes about six months for teenagers learning the guitar to reach a standard where they can play in front of a group. Of course this depends how much they practise.

A great idea is to convince someone who is a competent musician, perhaps even the new guitarist's teacher or an older person from church to play with the group while the young person is learning.

It is also important that someone who is sympathetic to church music teaches the young person and that he or she is experienced in leading congregational singing. They should not learn from the lead guitarist in the local music shop. Lead guitar is not what is needed – rhythm is much more important.

Consequently, acoustic guitars are best to learn on and lead singing with. The young person learning the instrument needs to understand that making a few mistakes with chords does not matter, rhythm matters. If you are not in time, it is difficult for the group to sing and follow the musician. A few wrong chords won't make the slightest difference.

A good tip is to throw the young learning guitarist into the deep end, that is, ask them to play 'unplugged' in the church band so they can gain some experience. The experience of being 'seen but not heard' will not only teach them some songs but also give them much needed experience in how to lead singing in church.

It is also worth thinking through singing without an instrument, that is, with a capable song leader using his/her voice only. However, be prepared. When it works, it works well. When it doesn't, it can be a disaster.

(You could try singing with backing music from a CD player, although I've always found this uninspiring.)

What if there is no one willing to lead singing?

If you have no one who is learning an instrument or shows any ability, there are a couple of things you can do. You can try to raise some money and buy a guitar. This will belong to the youth group and it will be there for anyone who comes along and wants to learn how to play it. I have found that if a guitar is available, quite often someone will give it a shot. Given the influence that music has today, you may find that with a bit of encouragement, there is someone willing to learn. You can also try to raise some money to give lessons to anyone who is willing to have a go. The last resort is for the leader to learn how to play. This may lead to a couple of young people following your example.

Choosing Songs

Once you have decided to take the plunge and sing, choosing the songs to sing is your next challenge. The main thing is not to make it too hard on the singers and new musician. Therefore choose songs with only a few chords that are easy to sing (and not too high for the young men in the group!).

There are a few interactive CDs around, which have some good songs. You can print out the music from enhanced CDs as well as play the song. This makes it easier to learn because the musician can play along with the song at home while they practise.

It is also good to pick songs that are fun. Don't begin with hymns. They are often too hard to sing (they have too many notes), and have difficult wording. If you love hymns, leave them for later on.

Practical Advice

Make sure the youth group is seated close together, so they can hear each other. This will encourage the people in the group not to feel as if they are the only ones trying to sing.

It is important that your leadership team is united in the desire to sing. Leaders are there to lead. This is imperative when it comes to singing. The leaders must sing with enthusiasm! This is really important, as they have to set the tone and be a good example. Leaders should not sit together, they should be spread out among the group.

Encourage the young men. For teenage boys using their voice can be a daunting experience, so encourage them to just have a crack at it (excuse the pun!).

Songs with actions and clapping can often help the enthusiasm, although it is also important not to take the focus away from what you are singing and to whom you are singing.

Finally, stay with it, it can be difficult at first but it is worthwhile. Just because the group won't sing the first time doesn't mean they will never sing. It could take months, but once you've made the decision, stay with it, for the rewards are great.

Basic steps to bring in singing

1. Find a musician who is willing and able to lead the singing.
2. Convince the group that it is worthwhile.
3. Choose some appropriate songs.
4. Introduce singing into the group.

(If you wish to contact Graham for more advice, he is happy for you to email him at gtsinging@yahoo.com.)

Our quest for better singing

Scott Tubman is a youth leader who left Australia to be trained and minister in Capetown, South Africa. He sent me some thoughts on bringing in better singing to his youth group, which I found very helpful.

After about a term of Youth Group it dawned on us that when we said, 'Time for singing!' we were kidding ourselves. The fact of the matter was that many of our kids simply didn't open their mouths and the rest were feeble at best. It was becoming a bit of an embarrassment and more to the point it began the meeting on a bad note (sorry about that!). We first thought that it was a purely musical problem. So we attacked it from this angle. We began by turning down the volume of the band so we didn't drown out any singing that was trying to get through. Not much response. We then decided to take the microphone away from our song leader so that the voices of the kids would fill the void and they would realize that they couldn't rely on the person up the front doing all the work. There was only marginal improvement.

It then dawned on me that our singing problem was not just a musical concern. In the wider context of our group, participation was at an all time low. People felt awkward sharing, praying and singing out loud. In other words, we had developed a spectator culture. We were doing all the right things, praying, sharing (or trying to!) having a good solid talk but there wasn't that vibe that got people excited about being there. Together with my leaders we developed the following graph. We then marked where we thought we were and where we wanted to be.

Crazy   Rowdy   Excited   Involved   Detached   Withdrawn   Passive   Numb   Dead

⟶

We decided that we were somewhere between detached and withdrawn. Our desire was to be up around the excited/involved end. The history of the group was that it used to be too rowdy and needed some 'taming'. This had happened although perhaps we tamed it too much. The question that faced us was: How do we move from passive to excited involvement?

All of a sudden our quest for better singing took on a whole new perspective. While improving the singing was still on the agenda, we saw it within the context of the whole meeting and had discovered a far greater issue. The kids needed to be brought from being detached to being involved. In light of these new discoveries we took the following action:

We changed the seating arrangement slightly.

We had fallen into almost a classroom situation, rows of chairs all facing the front. We changed to make it more like a mini amphitheatre, curving the rows into a horseshoe shape so that the kids could see each other thus increasing the sense of togetherness and community. People no longer felt like they were alone when they sang, prayed or shared. It also gave us the bonus of having a 'performance space' for skits or for the speaker to move about.

We changed the order of the programme

Instead of always finishing with a talk we threw in a song, instead of always starting with announcements we began by having some skits. We still included all the 'musts', but we mixed it up a bit. The kids felt comfortable with the meeting but never quite knew what was happening next. We also found it advantageous to begin with something that was quite interactive to set the tone for the meeting.

We included more interactive segments

We began more skits and came up with more creative ways to do the old segments. They were big hits! But more importantly it got kids talking, laughing and interacting the way we wanted them to, not in a rowdy out of control kind of way.

We trained ourselves not to jump in and squash noise so quickly

We had become used to running quite a clinical meeting where everything had its place and everything ran without a hitch. We had to retrain ourselves to go with something that popped out of nowhere and to be more spontaneous.

We involved the young people more in the programme

We would have a quick Bible study review/interview or ask a kid to open or close in prayer. Without handing the meeting over to them we got them involved and increased their participation and ownership.

Because of some basic changes in our programme, we have seen a great improvement in all aspects of the meeting – including better singing.

(Scott is a very experienced youth leader and is happy for you to contact him at stubman@mweb.co.za).

CHAPTER 16

Food glorious food!

Every day they continued to meet together in the temple courts. They broke bread in their homes and ate together with glad and sincere hearts ... (Acts 2:46)

A quick look at the New Testament will reveal that eating a meal together was high on the list of activities of Jesus and members of the early church. Jesus ate with various people (Matthew 26:26; Mark 2:16; Luke 11:37; Luke 14:1) and one of the characteristics of the early church was 'breaking bread in their homes and eating together' (Acts 2:46). Therefore, why not make this a feature of your youth group's time together? Furthermore, I probably don't need to remind you of this, kids love to eat!

At the beginning of the meeting

Put out some light snacks for when the kids first gather together. This will give them a 'gathering point' where they can stand around and catch up on each other's week. Give them plenty of time to talk (15 to 30 minutes). This is a good time for leaders to mingle and catch up as well. They can also meet newcomers.

At the end

Most meetings finish with food. Why not think about regularly eating together afterward? Ask some parents or older people in your congregation to prepare something that is cheap, easy and tasty. A meal gives group members time to grow in their relationships with each other and to talk about the time they have just spent together in youth group.

A youth dinner

From time to time make a full meal the main focus of youth group programme. You can pray around the tables, and have a Bible study on an appropriate theme (Christian fellowship, Jesus being the bread of life etc.). With a bit of creativity you could even have a BRW, Bible game or Spotlight during the meal together. To make the meal even better, have large bowls and plates of food on the table so that the kids have to serve each other.

CHAPTER 17

Notices/announcements

Key thought:	Announcements can be an important time to prepare the group for upcoming events. However, the way information flows from leader to young person can usually be improved.

Most of us have sat through a flurry of announcements at meetings. Usually they are about an upcoming event or registrations that are due for something taking place in a few weeks. We may even have joked about announcements taking longer than the Bible talk. Announcements are an important part of the programme and there are a few things we can do to make them more effective.

Ways to make announcements more effective

Ask yourself, 'Is this announcement really necessary?'

Quite often it isn't. In fact, many apply only to a select group of individuals within the group. If this is the case you often alienate (or bore) the rest of the group while you talk to the smaller subgroup. Can you make this announcement when the other group is not present? You might ask them to come and see you after the programme (or while food is being served). If your group is small, gather the select group before or after the meeting and make the announcement personally.

Have a monthly calendar

If you are able, at the beginning of each month send or hand out to the group a monthly calendar with every event clearly marked. You can include reminders of upcoming events at the bottom of the page as well as birthdays and other interesting events.

Email/Website/Letters

Collect everyone's email address and send notices electronically. You can also have the announcements posted on your website (Do you have a website? If not, correct this straight away. There must be someone in your group who can build one fairly quickly.) There is also 'snail mail'. Kids love to receive letters. Send them everything they need to know by mail each month. (We do this in addition to emails and our website.)

Make announcements in your small groups

Make sure that your small group leaders know about any announcements that need to be made. They can give notice of these in their weekly gathering. This is a more effective way of communicating announcements than standing up in front of the main group.

Creative ways to do announcements

Video

Here's an experiment. Stand up and make the announcements that you had planned to give. Before the next week's programme rolls around, spend a few minutes videoing the same announcements. Then show the video to the group. You may find that they sit there riveted as they watch the video of you giving the very same notices! It may be an indictment on today's culture (or the way we give announcements) but it can be much more effective to use a youth friendly format to convey information. With a bit of creativity, it can also be more entertaining.

Have a newsreader

Every now and then ask a leader/young person to play the role of newsreader to give the notices. They can have 'special reports' and even a weather forecast for the upcoming event. This could prove to be effective and a lot of fun.

Have the kids make the announcements

Instead of standing up and announcing a forthcoming camp, form the young people into small groups and have *the young people* give the announcement. They can do this by putting together short skits or simply standing and speaking. Once we broke the group into smaller groups and gave them a few minutes to prepare an announcement for our upcoming camp. However, they had to do this 'cheer leader style'! After a short time of preparation, they advertised the camp by jumping around and cheering in unison like cheerleaders. This was much more effective than the leader standing up and droning on. On several occasions, we asked a couple of young people to stand up and give a 20 second 'impassioned' speech to persuade the group to come to the social event in a couple of weeks. It was great fun.

Weekly Bible studies

The one announcement you must make each week is the weekly Bible studies (if you have them). These are a pivotal part of your youth programme. Therefore, make sure you let everyone know that they are on each week.

Putting it all together

Guidelines for running an effective weekly gathering/meeting

Make sure there is a nice sense of 'flow'

If you include a mixer activity, the next segment should be something that is active like a memory verse. Don't put things back to back that don't go together. An Operation World can be followed by a prayer time, but not something rowdy. In other words, look at the components of your programme beforehand and ensure that they fit together well.

Have one main leader

It is important that one person holds the whole thing together. This person will lead from the front, begin the meeting, welcome everyone and get the programme started. This main leader will also make sure that everything fits together and runs smoothly. This doesn't mean that he or she will run everything. Other leaders and kids will run some of the segments. The main leader is merely responsible for keeping the whole thing together.

(NB: While it is a good idea to have a variety of people introducing and running the various segments, don't have too many people coming to the front as it can become too crowded.)

Give the leader of each segment (or the whole meeting) time to develop and learn

Some leaders find that standing up in front of a group is an unnerving experience. It is important that they have time to learn the art of leading an activity or segment. Therefore, it may be helpful to give them a three-week stint. Ask a leader or young person to run a prayer time for three weeks in a row. If the first week doesn't go so well, this gives them time to try again and hopefully they will do it better.

HOT TIP It may be helpful to invite an 'expert' at the beginning of the year to provide some training in public speaking skills. At one church, we had a well-known news reader, who is also a keen Christian, give us two hours of practical instruction on how to conduct yourself in front of a crowd. It was a huge help.

Use this time to train new leaders

Following on from the previous idea, encourage newer leaders and the young people to try leading their favourite programme segments. This shares the load and develops leadership for the future.

Keep your eye on the clock. Don't go too short! Don't go too long!

Each group will no doubt have its own time constraints and reasons for why it meets when it does.

Too short!

Many groups try to cram everything into an hour or less. This is difficult if you are having a solid time in the Bible. We have found that if we are having Bible study (or discussion groups), a prayer time and a few other segments, then we must plan for an hour and fifteen minutes to an hour and a half. Some groups that meet on a Sunday before the evening church service find they have to leave some segments out of the programme (or they rush along at a frantic pace). This is a shame. Avoid this trap by beginning a bit earlier!

Too long!

While it is helpful to have a good amount of time up your sleeve, be careful that you don't have so much time that things begin to drag. If your meetings are too long, either shorten them or have a time for food and chatting afterwards. Most kids will love some time just to 'hang around'.

Organising the Meeting

First decide the outcome you expect for the weekly meeting. What is it you hope to accomplish? Do you want to have one theme that permeates every segment (and ties in to the talk/study)? Or are you happy to have a number of helpful items that may not link up thematically but are helpful nonetheless? Both are acceptable.

Step 1

Make a list of the *musts* for all meetings, for example:

Welcome
Announcements
Weekly Bible study reminders
Prayer Time
Bible study
Close
(Snacks/ dinner?)

WHAT IS THE *GOAL* OF THE MEETING?

WHAT ARE THE THINGS YOU *MUST* DO?

WHAT ARE SOME THINGS YOU *CAN* DO?

Step 2

Add any items that are *musts* but only for that week (for instance an advertisement for the camp to be held in a few weeks, meeting new leaders etc.).

Step 3

List the things you can do that week, such as Spotlight or Biblical Secret Sound. Some of these may be things you did last week and you wish to carry over (Q&A for instance). Or they may be things that you haven't done for a while and are ready to bring back (such as Spotlight).

Step 4

Combine the two lists. Some things you will do once only, others you may do a few weeks in a row.

I will try to repeat things we 'can do' a few weeks in a row. If we are having a testimony or sharing what we have read that week from the Bible, it can be helpful to do it two or three times so the kids can come prepared for the next week.

It is helpful to realise that some of the 'can do' activities can be a bit rowdy. Therefore I will plan appropriately and follow a rowdy activity with a more mellow segment. For instance, if we are having skits based around our memory verse, I will then think about moving into an Operation World or Favourite Tune before we have a prayer time or the main talk.

In short, the time should open with something that reflects the fact that you are a group of people who follow Jesus. Therefore, begin with a welcome, a prayer and maybe some type of light sharing question to begin the programme. Then, move into a fun and helpful activity such as a Bible game or memory verse. Then move on to a sharing time – things like Q&A, testimonies, what you've been reading in the Bible etc. Then have a time of prayer and looking at the Bible (talk, discussion groups). If it is appropriate, have some singing at the beginning and something to eat at the end.

> **A typical weekly youth meeting will look something like this:**
>
> **A welcome that pulls the group together at the start**
> **A Christian activity that is fun and helpful**
> **A time of Christian sharing**
> **Prayer**
> **Bible study**
> **Finish**

Musts	A good clear *Welcome* • A time of group *Prayer* • A *Bible talk or study* • A *close* to the meeting (prayer)
Cans	Sharing question (skits on sharing question) • Singing • Spotlight • Bible Game • Memory Verse • Bible Sharing (BRW) • Q&A • Jesus Freak • Scalpel • Testimony/Testify • Favourite Song • Predicament • Operation World • Notices/announcements • Discussion groups • Food
Rowdy items	Sharing question • Skits • Spotlight • Bible Game • Memory Verse • Predicament • Notices/announcements if you did skits
Group sharing items	Welcome Sharing question • Bible Sharing (BRW) • Q&A • Testimony/Testify • Favourite Tune • Predicament • Operation World • Prayer Time

An 8-Week Programme

Here is an outline for a suggested programme that will last for approximately a term. The length of each meeting will vary depending on a number of factors (size of the group, number of leaders etc.). You may need to cut out some segments. I have included a memory verse for most weeks because we do it every week in our group.

(This programme assumes people are seated in a semi-circle facing a whiteboard. If you had to, you could also seat everyone on the floor. Alternatively, you could begin the programme in a larger area and have a welcome and open in prayer, run the first activity and then move to a smaller area with chairs set up where you would start with a sharing question).

WEEK 1

Welcome
Each week we will begin with either a sharing question or a dramatic answer to a question. These might be based on current happenings (the past week/future weekend), or something related to the talk. Please refer to the list of Spotlight/Sharing questions in the resource section for help.

Opening prayer

Mixer Game
Find your match.

Spotlight
This will be done 'Classic Style'. That is, one interviewer, one person spotlighted. A short prayer will be said for the person spotlighted.

Bible game
Fill in the Blanks. This will introduce our memory verse.

Memory Verse
As we have just introduced it in the game, this will be brief. The leader of the game will repeat the verse a few times and do it 'Characters'.

Testimony
A leader or other member of the group will share their testimony. (N.B. We may not have time to do this.)

Prayer Time
Group prayer. Thanks/Help.

Talk/Bible study (discussion groups)

Close

WEEK 2

Welcome
(This is up to the leader. It will be either a short introduction or a sharing question.)

Opening prayer

Spotlight
This will be done 'Tag team'. I will have two leaders (or a leader and a young person) choose a person and each will ask three questions. One person will ask 'light questions' the other will ask more serious ones. A short prayer will be said for the person spotlighted.

Memory Verse

We will do this verse 'first letter revision' style. (This is where you write the verse up on the board giving only the first letter of each word. You have teams who have to figure out either the whole verse or certain lines of the verse.)

Testimony

A leader or other member of the group will share their testimony. (I will then tell the group that next week it is 'your turn'!)

Prayer Time

Group prayer. Thanks/Help.

Talk/Bible study (discussion groups)

Close

WEEK 3

Welcome

(This is up to the leader. It will be either a brief introduction or a sharing question.)

Opening prayer

Spotlight

This will be done either 'Classic' style or 'The Talk Show'.

Memory Verse

We will do this 'Memory verse circle' style. This is where the group sits in a circle and certain word/s are allocated to each chair. At various times we will move the group a few chairs to the left. We will use a stopwatch to time this and we will try to do it with our eyes closed. When this is done, I will ask volunteers to say the verse word perfect.

Testimony (Impromptu Testimony Time)

The group will be asked if anyone wants to give their testimony. We might go into a time of general testifying as to what God is doing in our lives.

Prayer Time

We will share prayer points and pray in small groups

Talk/Bible study (discussion groups)

Close

WEEK 4

Welcome

(This is up to the leader. It will be either a short introduction or a sharing question.)

Opening prayer

Bible Game
1. Celebrity Tic Tac Toe. I will use questions from the previous study series and the memory verse from the last three weeks. Or,
2. Bible Freeze Frames.

Q&A

Operation World

Prayer Time
We will take prayer points / requests in concentric circles (Outer circle= the world, inner circle = Australia, smallest circle = us).

Talk/Bible study (discussion groups)

Close

WEEK 5

Welcome:
(This is up to the leader. It will be either a short introduction or a sharing question.)

Opening prayer

Bible Game
Bible Blanks

Memory Verse/ Bible Game
We will introduce the verse 'Head Buzzer' style. We will have various pairs who will answer questions. This will slowly reveal the verse up on the whiteboard. First to guess the verse wins.

Q&A

Operation World
A member of the group will give a brief report on a country that we will pray for in the prayer time.

Prayer Time
Group prayer. Thanks/Help.

Talk/Bible study (discussion groups)

Close

WEEK 6

Welcome

(This is up to the leader. It will be either a short introduction or a sharing question.)

Opening prayer

Memory Verse

We will do skits on the verse. We will either give each group a theme to run with (cowboys and indians, gangster, mad scientist) or ask them to present it in a musical style (opera, rap etc.). This will take some time. Therefore, we will not have a Bible game.

Flag/Testify/BRW

We will ask for people in the group to come up and share what they have been learning from their Bibles. We will also have time to share either how we have given a witness for Christ or what God has been doing in our lives.

Prayer Time

We will pray in small groups.

Talk/Bible study (discussion groups)

Close

(During this programme I will have a Secret Bible Sound played at various times until someone guesses it.)

WEEK 7

Welcome

(This is up to the leader. It will be either a short introduction or a sharing question.)

Opening prayer

Spotlight

Done 'Classic' style.

Memory Verse

This will be done review fashion (word relay, jigsaw puzzle, memory verse statues, word for word competition).

Flag/Testify/BRW

We will ask for people in the group to come up and share what they have been learning from their Bibles. We will also have time to share either how we have given a witness for Christ or what God has been doing in our lives.

Prayer Time

Group prayer. Thanks/Help.

Talk/Bible study (discussion groups)

Close

(During this programme I will have a Secret Bible Sound played at various times until someone guesses it.)

N.B. I might replace Flag/Testify/BRW with either Scalpel or Predicament.

WEEK 8

Welcome

(This is up to the leader. It will be either a short introduction or a sharing question.)

Opening prayer

Predicament

We will set a predicament and then give the young people the opportunity to act out or give some answers. We will then provide some Bible verses that shed some light on the situation. This may take some time as it could lead to a lively discussion. With this in mind, I have not included a Bible game or sharing time in the programme.

Prayer Time

I will split the whiteboard in three sections: global, national, local. We will take prayer requests and pray as a group.

Talk/Bible study (discussion groups)

Close

During this programme I will have a Secret Bible Sound played at various times until someone guesses it.

Some last thoughts

1. There will be some change to this programme depending on the success or failure of some of the segments. If one segment goes well and takes more time, this may mean we drop something and slot it in next week. An example of this is Q&A. If it goes well, you may wish to give it more time.

2. I will adapt to changes in the programme. For instance, if someone arrives that night wishing to play a 'Favourite Tune', I will accommodate that, which may mean that I have to drop something out of the programme.

3. It may be helpful to cut down some of the contents in one of the later weeks and have dinner together. During this dinner you could have your prayer time and give a short devotion or teaching segment. You could include a testimony or sharing time as well. Depending on your group and the seating arrangements, you could have

impromptu dramas presented by each table. These dramas could be on the evening's subject or a memory verse review.

4. I might change the programme one week and run it completely differently. For instance, we have run our whole meeting around the game Quiz Show. We set up the whiteboard with a list of categories at the top (Old Testament/New Testament/People in youth group/Past Youth Group Events/Memory Verses). Under these headings were a number of envelopes with various numerical values (Old Testament for 100/200/300 etc). In each envelope was either a relevant question on the topic or a segment that we had planned to do (prayer/memory verse/BRW etc.). This has proved to be a lot of fun and a nice change.

CHAPTER 19

Setting the scene

Most of us have little control over the premises we use. The church hall may be perfect. Or it may be too big, old and cold or unfriendly in some other way. It may have been built to withstand the bombs of World War 1 or built to house the growth that never came.

Whatever the case, it is important that your group is as comfortable as it can be. To get the most out of your meeting place there are some basic steps that can ensure it works for us and not against us.

Is your building 'youth friendly'?

Can you use the building to run the type of programme that you want? Will somebody be upset if you move things around? Many youth groups have had a rocky relationship with the rest of the church because of a clash of expectations over how the building will be used.

Make sure you discuss how you want to use the building with the senior minister and relevant people.

Climate control

Many a meeting has been spoiled because the room is too hot or stuffy. Make sure there is adequate ventilation. Is it too hot? See if you can raise some money for some fans to help circulate the air. Is it too cold? Try to get some heaters. You can have the kids sit on couches or soft chairs with blankets. This is warmer but can often make the group too comfortable. Another thing you can do is to include a break for a hot drink during the programme. The best solution is to plead with the minister/elders to spend some money on heaters or central heating. Be careful about heating up the building too much. A group of rowdy teenagers has a way of raising the temperature without the need for too much heating.

Check the lighting

Most buildings have overhead fluorescent lights. This is not a disaster but make sure that they all work and there is enough light. You don't want the kids to start bringing miner's hats complete with lamps to youth group. If the lighting is too bright, you may want to invest in some lights that throw the light upwards. This gives a more gentle, softer light, yet is still effective.

The seating

There are many common mistakes when it comes to arranging seating. Some groups let the young people flop down wherever they want to. This usually ends up with kids scattered everywhere, which is not conducive to building a group. Other groups sit in rigid rows staring at the back of each other's heads. This is hardly a positive social experience. Some groups sit in a circle. This is good for some segments of your programme but not for others. (It is also uncomfortable for the newcomer.)

My suggestion is to arrange the seats in a curve, something like an amphitheatre. This means that attention is focused on the action, but they can also see most other people in the group without too much difficulty. My rule of thumb is that from any given seat, the person should be able to see around two thirds of the group.

Keep in mind that seating will need to be flexible depending on the programme. If you are doing skits or a memory verse game you will need to be able to change the seating quickly.

What if the building is too big?

Many groups meet in a hall that can comfortably fit 60 kids. The problem is that there are only ten people in the group. If you can't find a smaller meeting place, the next best thing is to find some office partitions or dividers. You can use these to partition a corner of the building to making it nice and cosy. These are often advertised for sale in the newspaper or at auction houses selling office furniture.

You can divide the hall in two. When the kids walk in you can have one half set up for food or to hang around chatting. When that is done, move them into the second part of the hall that is set up for the meeting. A variation of this is to set up the first half of the hall for a game or sharing time. The seats may be set up in a circle. When this is done, move them into another half with different seating for the talk or next part of the programme.

The joy of the whiteboard

It has been my experience that a large whiteboard can make your life a lot easier. Chalkboards are okay, but only just. They are messy and some nut will always scrape his fingernails along the surface to get a reaction from the girls. Overhead projectors are suitable but difficult to operate unless you have handwriting like your fifth grade English teacher. These days, it is either the whiteboard or a video projector. So far, I haven't been able to convince the elders of my desperate need for a video projector (they are more concerned with buying Bibles or feeding the poor. Where are their priorities?)

Use nonpermanent marking pens, or you'll spend hours cleaning the whiteboard. You will also need to be prepared. Many programmes have been interrupted because we have misplaced our whiteboard pen. I buy them by the dozen and always keep a few in my car or Bible cover.

Bibles

You must have Bibles ready to be passed around for a Bible game or the talk later on. Or better yet, have them placed on or under each seat.

Finally, always arrive with enough time before the meeting to set up everything and to make sure you have everything you need. You should also spend some time in prayer. I like to sit in the quiet building in silent contemplation before the weekly hurricane arrives.

The straw removal system

Some of us have had a hard time introducing changes to our programme. There is resistance from leaders, elders or the kids. This is understandable and not unusual. If you find that trying to bring in change is about as welcome as a visit to the dentist, there are some things you can do.

Ways to introduce change

1. Work slowly

I realise that some of you come from a tradition of rowdy, unproductive games (straw) and a short Bible talk with little else. The programme I have suggested may come as quite a shock to the group. If this is the case, here's what I'd do: I would begin with a welcome, sharing question and a prayer to kick off the night. I would then spend 10 minutes playing a mindless game or two (this causes me pain to even suggest it but anyway...). I would then move into a rowdy Bible game or memory verse. Depending on the length of the meeting, you could either do both or alternate between Bible games and memory verse activities. (For three weeks have some Bible games, for the next three weeks do a memory verse.) I would then have a Spotlight. After a few weeks introduce testimonies from leaders or members of the church. We would also have a prayer time each week followed by the usual Bible study or discussion groups. I would introduce a regular prayer time even if there is resistance from some of the members of the group. Prayer is a non-negotiable part of the Christian youth group. A few months later I would introduce some sort of sharing time (I.T.T.'s, Testify etc.). The leaders will need to set the tone for this to work well. I would aim to hold a camp or overnight. This brings about better relationships. My goal is to move the group away from the straw after a period of time (three to six months?).

The straw removal system would look something like this:

Immediately

Welcome / Prayer / Sharing Question or dramatic answer to question / straw game(s) / Bible game or Memory verse / Spotlight / Prayer time / Bible talk / food / close.

A few weeks later

Keep the same pattern yet drop Spotlight (for a few weeks) / Introduce sharing time (leaders may need to get things started) / Q&A.

Later (three months or after a camp)

Remove straw. Have food, music and mingling for 15–20 minutes. The goal is to strive for an enjoyable programme filled with solid Christian content and good relationships. If this is completed successfully, I would take my wife out to an expensive restaurant, kiss any strangers I met, take in the nearest stray dog, mow all my neighbour's lawns and fall on my knees in thankful prayer.

It may also be helpful to run your 'rowdy' time in one part of the hall (or room) and then move to another when you are trying to settle things down a bit. It is amazing how a small thing like a change of scenery can affect a group.

2. Build a group based around good relationships

I would make sure that I have activities that promote community and good relationships. This means that I would have small groups up and running along with a camp or two.

3. Introduce new ideas at a camp

Hold a camp built around a number of new programming ideas. If the camp works, you can easily include the new ideas (which will no longer be new) in the weekly meeting.

4. Have a month of change

Tell the kids that this month will be 'Youth group with a twist!' or something of the kind. During this month bring in Bible games, memory verses and sharing questions.

5. Prayer and Bible study

Pray heartily that God will warm the hearts of all involved to accept changes that will bring spiritual growth and loving relationships. Spend time in Bible study with your leaders and the young people in the group. Look at sections of the Bible such as Acts 2:42–47. Spend time discussing how your group can be stronger and more loving. This may warm them to be more accepting of change. I would also regularly spend time with my leaders focussing our creative juices on developing a programme that is fun without the need for mindless straw. It may be helpful to have a leaders' day away every now and then to do this.

6. Flow

Remember the concept of 'flow'. Each year you will be moving kids up from the Sunday School, Kids Club or junior youth group into the following group. Your job will be much easier if the kids from the younger group have been in a programme built on good Christian content.

When they move up they will expect a programme based on Christian principles such as fellowship, prayer and Bible study, rather than straw.

Change will come much more easily if you have good programming for the junior or younger youth group, if there is one, if not, bring change to the Sunday School or Kids Club. (For a full explanation of the concept of flow see *Changing the World*, page 36.)

You are running a programme for young people to become strong Christians and stay strong for life. While there may be resistance on the part of the older kids, you may find that the younger ones are more accepting. As they move on to the older group (flow into it) they will bring their expectations with them and assume that the older group has good, solid content.

Naming programme segments

We have used names like Operation World and BRW for some years. Some of them date from the 1980s! If you feel that your group would balk at calling something 'Spotlight', think of a title that is more suitable for your setting. This may be the case for some of the Bible games we have suggested. You may need to change their names to make them more appropriate to your group.

HOT TIP Small groups

Most 'successful' youth groups will have a network of small group Bible studies at their core. These small groups (or cells) promote discipleship, help build strong relationships and go a long way toward making the weekly gathering more effective. (See *Changing the World*, p77.)

There may be some of you who have read the last few chapters and decided that you just don't have the gifts or personality to run these types of activities. If that is you, remember:

Practice makes perfect

Stay with it. Many of us have struggled at first.

Gather up other leaders who can help you

Iron sharpens iron! If you know another leader or a group of leaders, work with them and help each other to run these activities better.

Develop future leaders

Spend time developing those young people in your programme who will be confident to run a programme like this in the future. Begin now. A young person from the group can successfully run many (if not most) of these ideas. It may be your job to do no more than develop leaders for the future. They will be the people who will run a group that effectively builds strong disciples, reaches out to their friends and stays around for the long term. Hopefully this book will help you to reach this very important goal.

When all else fails there are three things any leader must do:

Honour God. You are not there to run a whiz-bang programme or to draw thousands of kids to the church. Ultimately you are there to give God the glory and honour that is due to him. I hope the activities in this book will help your group to do that.

Love the kids. Let the young people in your group know that they are important to you and always try your best to show them love.

Build for the future. Set the tone for youth group. That is, youth group is seen by all as a place to grow in the knowledge and love of Jesus. It is also a place of Christian community and love. From this group (with God's help) will come leaders who will keep the whole thing going.

C H A P T E R   2 1

Be patient

Hopefully the previous pages have given you some ideas for doing more effective ministry. However, some of you may be thinking, 'I don't know if I can do this.' Others will make changes to the programme that will cause the numbers to fall. Some of the kids who are used to a Christian youth group being a place of 'lots of entertainment, a little Christ' will leave for greener pastures (in reality those pastures aren't green, they are the colour of death).

It is important for you to be committed to this model of ministry for the long-term. Are you doing ministry that will impact kids for a few weeks or for a lifetime? It is of the utmost importance that you establish a ministry that will have a solid and lasting impact. Please do not fall into the trap of seeing success in terms of numbers. God doesn't see things this way and neither should you. God wants disciples who are committed to him, not fickle crowds who will move on (see Matthew 7:13–14; 7:21; Mark 8:34–38; John 6:60–70).

Be patient. It will take time for the changes you make to take root and grow. You may see your group shrink from 20 to eight. Hopefully, and with God's help, you can build these eight into people who love God and each other and are also eager to change the world for Jesus. With time, these eight young people will reach out to their friends, which may grow your group to 10. You will also be preparing the young people to be leaders in the future. In time, there will be a bigger leadership team that can run more small groups. Over several years this original group of eight may grow into a group of 20 or 30 people. These young people however, are not the good time crowd, only there to take what they can. They are there for Christian fellowship and because they are committed to the King. In time there will be a number of newcomers who have been brought by a friend to hear about Jesus.

In summary, view the youth group as a long-term project. While you are helping to lead it, do everything to make sure it has a lasting impact on the lives of those who attend. When you move on, hopefully there will be leaders whom you have trained to take over. They will continue the process of running a group devoted to building strong disciples who are equipped to reach out effectively. Remember, the big church down the road didn't appear overnight; it took years to develop (maybe even decades).

Example

It always encourages me to think of one youth leader who spent ten years slowly and faithfully discipling the young people in his group. Other groups around him appeared more impressive with larger numbers. He continued faithfully teaching kids to love Jesus, depend on him in prayer, and to love each other. At the end of ten years he left a solid youth group of around 20 young people. It was not a huge youth group, but a strong one. Some of these young people went into full-time ministry; others stayed and took over the reins of the group. There are now about 80 young people in the group and it is going as strong as ever. What a great picture of effective youth ministry.

Be patient.

Good ministry takes time.

Build something that will last.

Build young people who will show the light of Christ to their friends.

Produce young people who will become leaders when they are older.

Stay with it!

Mixer games/activities

(These are helpful for positive relating but are not Bible games.)

Portrait Bingo

Give each person a 'Bingo sheet'. This is a piece of paper laid out as a grid with a question in each square of the grid. The goal of the game is to find someone who can answer the question or statement in the box. For example, you might have the statement, 'Find someone with an older sister', or, 'Find someone who went to the beach during the school holidays'. Once you have found a person who fulfils the category, you draw a picture of them in the square provided. (Each square needs to be fairly large to accommodate a drawing.)

Running this mixer

People move around asking others in the group if one of the questions is relevant to them. When they find someone who matches the description, they draw the face of the person in the box beside that question. The goal is to complete the page with faces drawn next to each question. Once finished you may like to see if people can identify every face drawn in the spaces. The same person's face can appear once only. You may wish to include two or three questions in the bottom of each box to help the group get to know each other better (favourite food, movie etc.).

Sample questions:
Someone who uses Colgate toothpaste
Someone who has a dog
Someone with red hair
Someone who has a brother
Someone who is 14 years old
Someone who likes soccer
Someone who loves chocolate
Someone who has a sister
Someone who has just started high school
Someone who has a cat
Someone who hates peas
Someone who loves school

Face drawing game

The group sits in a circle. Write everyone's name on a piece of paper and place the names in a hat or bowl. Give each person a piece of paper (A4 size) and a pen or pencil. Each person draws a name out of the hat—they are not to tell anyone whose name. When everyone has a name, they draw the face of the person whose name they have received, without anyone knowing who they are drawing. When everyone has finished, the person running the game collects the portraits and shows them one at a time to the group. The group tries to guess who is the subject of the drawing and who drew the picture. This game is a lot of fun.

Find your match

Ask a series of questions to form pairs in the group. Once people are in pairs, ask a question that both people must answer. You then ask volunteers to give their partner's answer.

Running this mixer

The leader stands on a chair and shouts out, 'Find someone who has the same hair colour as you.' The people in the group look for someone whose hair colour matches theirs. Allow them time to find someone. (Make sure everyone is paired.) Tell them to introduce themselves to each other and then ask, 'What has been the best thing you have done in the past week?' After a minute or two, ask for a few volunteers to report their partner's answer.

Repeat this using the 'matching' and sharing questions below. Make sure that people match with a different person each time. Pair up people without partners before asking the sharing question.

Find someone who:
Has the same hair colour
Has the same colour eyes
Is the same height
Was born in same month
Had the same breakfast
Has the same shoe size

Some sharing questions
What is the best gift you have every received?
If you could live anywhere for one year where would it be?
Which armed force would you join, army, navy or air?
Who is someone you admire?
What would you like to have done by age 50?
What is one question you would like to ask God?

Concentric Circles

Ask everyone to choose a partner and have the whole group sit in two concentric circles (one circle inside another). One partner sits on the inside circle facing out, and the other sits on the outer circle facing in (they are facing each other). Ask the group a question. For example, 'If you could visit anywhere for a month, where would you go and why?' The partners share their answer. (Once they have finished telling each other their answers, ask for a couple of volunteers to tell the group what their partner told them.)

Ask the people in the outside circle to move (for example, move three places clockwise, or five places anti-clockwise) so they are facing a new partner, then repeat the process. If you wish, you can alternate moving the outside circle and the inside circle. This is a fun way to mix and talk. It may be helpful to begin with a number of 'lighter' questions and gradually add more serious ones.

A variation: Musical Concentric Circles

Instead of sitting, run this mixer standing up. One circle stands inside the other with each person facing his/her partner. Play some music and have each circle move. The inside circle moves clockwise, the outer circle moves counter clockwise. When the music stops, they introduce themselves to their new partner and the leader sets a question for them to answer.

Name game

Have the group sit in a circle. One person begins by saying his or her name as well as the name of a fruit that starts with the same letter. For example, 'My name is Stephen and I like strawberries.' Then the next person repeats the previous person(s) name and their fruit and adds his or her name and what fruit goes with the name. (For example: 'His name is

Stephen and he likes strawberries, my name is Andrew and I like apples!) Continue until everyone in the circle has had a turn.

(You can vary the subject from fruit to vegetables, sports etc)

Your Name

Ask everyone in the group to say their full name and the reason why they have those names. There may be no other reason than their parents like them. But for most people at least one of their names is after someone in the family. This game gives each person the chance to find out a little bit more about other people in the group. (This will work best in a small group. If you have a large youth group you may want to break into smaller groups.)

Spotlight and sharing questions

Here are some sample questions you can ask during Spotlight or as an opening question for your meeting.

Information gathering questions

1. Full name, age, school and year at school. Does your middle or last name have any special meaning?

2. How many people are in your family? (How many of them are Christians?)

3. When you get dressed in the morning and you're putting on your socks, do you put the sock on your left or right foot first? (We always put them on the same foot first.)

4. Do you wet the toothbrush before or after you put on the toothpaste?

5. What is your favourite pizza topping?

6. Your parents have gone out for the evening and they leave you $20 for dinner. What do you buy for dinner with the money?

7. When you are at home studying, what CD would you be listening to?

8. If your radio had to be stuck on one station for a year, which station would you choose?

9. What is your favourite thing to do in your spare time?

10. Where is your best scar and how did you get it?

11. You can be an astronaut, a mountain climber, a deep-sea diver or a Polar explorer. Which one would you choose?

12. You can be a great singer, painter, athlete or thinker. Which one will you be?

13. You can have: an expensive stereo, computer, television or a fancy bike. Which one are you going to take?

14. What was the first CD you ever bought /were given?

15. What is your favourite computer game?

Light / Humorous questions

1. The circus comes to town and you decide that you are bored with your life and are going to run away with the circus. What would you do in the circus?

2. You have gone to a village overseas to be a missionary. The chief of the village has invited you to have a meal with him. You sit down to dinner and they serve up the traditional dish of the tribe. It's 12 sheep eyeballs. If you don't eat the meal the chief will be highly offended. Your only choices are to eat the eyes or offend the chief. What will it be?

3. If you became a professional wrestler, what would your name be and what would your 'signature move' be? (Wrestlers often have a special, crazy move designed to beat their opponent.)

4. If you had to make up a word to describe yourself, what would it be? (This is a hard question.)

5. What is your school song? Can you sing it?

6. Have you ever met someone famous? Who was it?

7. Who is the most interesting person you have ever met?

8. Describe the perfect hamburger.

9. Describe your worst haircut.

10. What's the best 'wipe-out' you've ever had?

11. Name a song you used to sing as a child?

12. What is your favourite piece of clothing of all time?

13. Did you have a favourite teddy bear? What was his/her name? Why was it your favourite?

14. You can see any band or performer in concert. Who will it be?

15. What was the best pet you ever had?

16. Which is your favourite cartoon character?

17. f you could be any superhero, who would you be?

18. If you could have any pet in the world, what would you choose?

19. If you could have a holiday to any destination this summer, where would you go?

20. Who would be sitting in the seat next to you (if you could name anyone)?

21. What meal would you have if you knew it was going to be your last?

22. You can have five people over for dinner. They can be famous or from the past. Who would you invite?

23. If you had to be a plant, what plant would you be?

24. If you had to get a tattoo, what would it be?

25. What is your greatest sporting achievement?

More serious questions

1. What is your favourite subject at school?

2. What is your worst subject at school?

3. What is the best thing about coming to youth group for you?

4. What is the best thing about being a Christian for you?

5. What is one question you would like to ask God?

6. What is something you are looking forward to about heaven?

7. What is something that we can pray for you?

Bible game questions

General questions

1. Name three parables of Jesus.

2. Name three miracles of Jesus.

3. Who wrote the most books in the New Testament? *(Paul)*

4. What was Paul's name before he was converted? *(Saul)*

5. Name three Old Testament prophets. *(Look up Bible index from Isaiah to Malachi – but include guys who didn't write a book like Elijah, Elisha, Micaiah, Nathan etc)*

6. From the book of Daniel – Daniel and three friends – two famous stories: the friends were thrown into something and Daniel was thrown into something. Where were they thrown? *(Friends were thrown into fiery furnace [Daniel 3] and Daniel was thrown into lions' den [Daniel 6])*

7. Name the two books in Old Testament named after women. *(Ruth, Esther)*

8. Noah and Ark – there were two of every animal – how many clean animals? *(7)*

9. In the Garden of Eden there were two trees, one whose fruit they couldn't eat and one they could – which one could they eat? *(Tree of Life)*

10. & 11. Recite a memory verse other than John 3:16 *(x 2)*

12. Who wrote the book of Revelation? *(John)*

13. There are books with numbers in front of them – name three. *(See Bible index)*

14. A New Testament writer wrote two letters to a man called Theophilus – what were the two letters? HINT the writer was a doctor. *(Luke and Acts)*

15. Jesus' transfiguration – name one of the people who appeared with him. *(Moses and Elijah [Mark 9])*

16. Name five of the Ten commandments. *(See Exodus 20:1–17 or Deuteronomy 5:6–21)*

17. Name three of the plagues sent to Egypt. *(See Exodus 7–11: blood, frogs, gnats, flies, death of livestock, boils, hail, locusts, darkness, death of firstborn child)*

18. In which New Testament book can you read the story of a shipwreck? *(Acts 27:27–44)*

19. Five New Testament books start with T, name all five *(See Bible index: 1 Thessalonians – Titus)*

20. Which king built the temple in Jerusalem? *(Solomon)*

Jesus

1. What was the name of the man that Jesus raised from the dead? *(Lazarus, John 11:38–44)*

2. What was the name of Jesus' cousin? *(John The Baptist, Luke 1)*

3. In what town was Jesus born? *(Bethlehem, Luke 2:1–6)*

4. What was the name of the angel that came to tell Mary she was going to have a child? *(Gabriel, Luke 1:26–27)*

5. Who was the governor that sentenced Jesus to death? *(Pilate, Matthew 27:11-13)*

6. Where was Jesus when he was tempted for 40 days? *(The desert, Matthew 4:1)*

7. Where was Jesus when the soldiers came to arrest him? *(In the Garden of Gethsemane /Mount of Olives, Matthew 26:36–45 and Luke 22:39–46)*

8. Who owned the tomb that Jesus was buried in? *(Joseph from Arimathea, John 19:38)*

9. What did the wise men follow to find Jesus? *(A star, Matthew 2:2)*

10. According to John's gospel, what is the first miracle Jesus performed? *(The water into wine, John 2)*

11. In John's gospel Jesus said some 'I am' sayings about himself. Can you tell us one (or three) of them? *(I am the gate, I am the good shepherd [John 10:9,11]; I am the light of the world [John 8:12]; I am the resurrection and the life [John 11:25]; I am the way, the truth and the life [John 14:6]; I am the vine John [15:5]; I am the bread of life [John 6:35]; before Abraham was born, I am [John 8:58])*

12. What was Jesus doing when the soldiers came to arrest him? *(Praying, Matthew 26:36–45)*

13. On two occasions Jesus fed masses of people. Can you tell me the number of people Jesus feed at one of the times? *(5000 and 4000, Mark 6:30ff, 8:1ff)*

14. What did the shepherds see in the fields the night Jesus was born? *(Angels praising God, Luke 2:8–20)*

15. Who was the King at the time of Jesus' birth? *(King Herod, Matthew 2:1)*

16. Where did Jesus' parents come from? *(Nazareth in Galilee, Luke 1:26)*

17. What did Jesus do for the widow from Nain? *(Raised her son from the dead, Luke 7:11–17)*

18. What did Jesus know about the lady he met at the well? *(How many husbands she has had, John 4:16–18)*

19. Who helped Jesus carry his cross? *(Simon of Cyrene, Matthew 27:32)*

20. In which river was Jesus baptised? *(The Jordan, Matthew 3:13)*

21. Which country did Jesus' parents escape to after the birth of Jesus? *(Egypt, Matthew 2:13)*

22. In John chapter 3 we read about a Pharisee who came to talk to Jesus at night. What is this man's name? *(Nicodemus, John 3:1)*

23. What did Jesus say was easier than a rich man entering heaven? *(A camel to enter through the eye of a needle, Luke 18:25)*

24. When Jesus cast the demons out of the man who was possessed by many demons, where did the demons go? *(Into the pigs, Mark 5:11–13)*

25. Who was the woman who poured perfume on Jesus' feet? *(Mary, John 12:2–3)*

26. Where was Jesus when his parents thought they had lost him? *(In the Temple, Luke 2:41–52)*

The Disciples

1. Which disciple betrayed Jesus? *(Judas, Luke 22:1–6)*

2. Which disciple was a tax collector before following Jesus? *(Matthew, Matthew 9:9–13)*

3. How much money was Judas given to betray Jesus? *(30 silver coins, Matthew 26:15)*

4. Which disciples were with Jesus at the transfiguration? *(Peter, James and John, Matthew 17:1)*

5. Which disciple said that he would have to see the holes in Jesus' hands and side to believe he was alive? *(Thomas, John 20:24–25)*

6. Which disciple denied knowing Jesus? *(Peter, Mark 14:66–72)*

7. What happened to Judas after he betrayed Jesus? *(He hung himself, Matthew 27:5)*

8. Name the disciples who wanted to sit at the left and right of Jesus in heaven. *(James and John, Mark 10:35–37)*

9. Which disciple's mother in law did Jesus heal? *(Simon, Mark 1:30)*

10. Who were the sons of Zebedee? *(James and John, Mark 1:19)*

11. Name five of the 12 disciples. *(Simon, whom he named Peter, Andrew, James, John, Philip, Bartholomew, Matthew, Thomas, James, Simon called Zealot, Judas and Judas Iscariot, Luke 6:12–16)*

12. Who was Jesus talking to when he said 'get behind me Satan'? *(Peter, Matthew 16:23)*

13. Name one disciple who was a fisherman before following Jesus. *(Simon Peter, Andrew, James and John)*

14. Which disciple walked on water with Jesus? *(Peter, Matthew 14:28–31)*

People of the Old Testament

1. Which man was promised a son at a very old age? *(Abraham, Genesis 15)*

2. Can you name the three sons of Adam who are mentioned in the Bible? *(Cain, Abel, Seth, Genesis 4:1–2, 5:3)*

3. Who was the first king of Israel? *(Saul)*

4. Which man was swallowed by a big fish? *(Jonah)*

5. Name one man that was placed into the fiery furnace in the book of Daniel. *(Shadrach, Meshach and Abednego, Daniel 3)*

6. What was the name of the giant that David killed? *(Goliath)*

7. Name the judge who killed the fat king by stabbing him in the belly. *(Ehud)*

8. Isaac had twin sons – what were their names? *(Jacob and Esau)*

9. What was the name of Abraham's wife? *(Sarah or Sarai)*

10. What was the name of the man that built the first temple in Jerusalem? *(Solomon)*

11. What was the name of Isaac's wife? *(Rebekah)*

12. What was the name of Abraham's firstborn son? *(Ishmael)*

13. Name one of Jacob's sons. *(Reuben, Simeon, Levi, Judah, Issachar, Zebulan, Joseph, Benjamin, Dan, Naphtali, Gad, Asher)*

14. What was the name of Abraham's nephew? *(Lot)*

15. What was the name of the lady with whom David had an affair? *(Bathsheba)*

16. Who is the strongest man in the Old Testament? *(Samson)*

17. What was the name of Bathsheba's husband? *(Uriah)*

18. What was the name of Samuel's mother? *(Hannah)*

19. Which man was thrown into the lion's den? *(Daniel)*

20. Who was the man that the whole Israelite nation started with? *(Abraham/Abram)*

21. Who was the man who was sold as a slave by his brothers? *(Joseph)*

22. In whose house was Joseph a servant? *(Potiphar)*

23. Who was the man that rebuilt the temple when the Israelites returned from exile? *(Ezra)*

24. Which man rebuilt the city wall when the Israelites returned from exile? *(Nehemiah)*

25. Which man killed more in his death then when he was alive? *(Samson)*

26. Who is described as a hairy man? *(Esau)*

27. Who worked for seven years for the right to marry the woman he loved? *(Jacob)*

28. What was the name of the woman who killed a man by hammering a tent peg through his head? *(Jael)*

29. Who led the Israelites after Moses died? *(Joshua)*

30. What was the name of the woman who survived the fall of Jericho with her family? *(Rahab)*

31. Name the woman judge from the book of Judges. *(Deborah)*

32. Who was the wisest king in Israel's history? *(Solomon)*

33. Which queen came to visit Solomon because he was so wise? *(The Queen of Sheba)*

People in the New Testament

1. Who was the first man to be put to death because of his faith in Jesus? *(Stephen)*

2. Name the man who climbed a tree to see Jesus. *(Zacchaeus)*

3. Which man preached to the Ethiopian eunuch? *(Philip)*

4. What were the names of the couple that lied to Peter and died on the spot? *(Ananias and Sapphira)*

5. Who was chosen as the new disciple to replace Judas? *(Matthias)*

6. Name the man who was converted on the road to Damascus. *(Saul/Paul)*

7. Name the centurion who was sent to Peter to tell him about Jesus. *(Cornelius)*

8. Who did Paul have a disagreement with over taking Mark on a missionary trip? *(Barnabas)*

9. How did John the Baptist die? *(He was beheaded)*

10. Which Pharisee was a member of Jewish ruling council and came to visit Jesus at night? *(Nicodemus)*

11. What were the names of Lazarus' sisters? *(Mary and Martha)*

Events, Places and Other Stuff

1. Which woman was turned into salt when she looked back at the city of Sodom and Gomorrah? *(Lot's wife)*
2. Name the mountain that Moses went up to get the Ten commandments. *(Mt Sinai)*
3. What was the name of the country where the Israelites where slaves? *(Egypt)*
4. What was the name of the Promised Land before the Israelites occupied it? *(Canaan)*
5. Where were Peter and John heading when they healed the lame man in Acts 3? *(To the Temple to pray)*
6. What was the name of the sea that parted in two for the Israelites to walk through? *(The Red Sea)*
7. Which city and its walls fell down at the sound of a trumpet? *(Jericho)*
8. What was the name of the river the Israelites crossed before they entered the Promised Land? *(The Jordan)*
9. Where did Moses flee to? *(Midian)*
10. In which city did Paul deliver the sermon in the meeting of the Areopagus in Acts 17? *(Athens)*
11. In what country was Abraham living when God called Abraham to follow him? *(Egypt)*
12. Name the city where Jonah was to go and tell the people to repent. *(Ninevah)*
13. How many days were the Israelites told to walk around Jericho? *(7)*
14. On the last day the Israelites walked around Jericho, how many times did they have to walk around? *(7)*
15. What was the first plague God sent on Egypt? *(Blood)*
16. What was the last plague God sent on Egypt? *(The death of the firstborn)*
17. What kind of transport did Jonah use to flee from God? *(A boat)*

People who made mistakes or lacked faith in the Bible

1. Which Old Testament king had an affair with the women next door? *(David)*
2. Which man persecuted and put to death Christians before he was converted? *(Saul/Paul)*
3. Who were the first people to disobey God? *(Adam and Eve)*
4. Which man had 700 hundred wives and 300 concubines? *(Solomon)*
5. Name the woman who laughed when she was told she was going to have a baby. *(Sarah)*
6. Who deceived his brother out of his right to the first son's inheritance? *(Jacob)*
7. Who was the first man to get drunk in the Bible? *(Noah)*
8. Who was the first man to kill his brother? *(Cain)*

9. Name the man who told a woman the secret to his strength. *(Samson)*

10. Who denied knowing Jesus three times? *(Peter)*

11. Name the man who betrayed Jesus. *(Judas)*

Book of the Bible

1. What's the last book in the Old Testament? *(Malachi)*

2. Name the four gospels. *(Matthew, Mark, Luke, John)*

3. Which books did the disciple John write? *(John, 1,2 and 3 John, Revelation)*

4. In which book of the Bible do you find the shortest verse? *(John 11:35)*

5. Which is the longest book in the Bible? *(Psalms)*

6. What book comes after Isaiah? *(Jeremiah)*

7. Luke wrote two books, what are their names? *(Luke, Acts)*

8. Name the first and last books of the Bible. *(Genesis, Revelation)*

9. How many books in the Old Testament? *(39)*

10. How many books in the New Testament? *(27)*

11. In which book do you read about the Israelites entering into the Promised Land? *(Joshua)*

12. In which New Testament book do you read about the spread of the gospel? *(Acts)*

13. How many psalms in the book of Psalms? *(150)*

14. Who wrote the book of Proverbs? *(Solomon)*

15. Where was John when he wrote the book of Revelation? *(In prison on the island of Patmos)*

16. In which book do you read about the conversion of Paul? *(Acts)*

17. Which book is about a woman who becomes a queen and saves the lives of her fellow Jews? *(Esther)*

18. Name the first five books of the Bible. *(Genesis, Exodus, Leviticus, Numbers, Deuteronomy)*

19. In which book do you read about the Exodus? *(Exodus)*

20. In which book of the Bible do we read about the creation of the world? *(Genesis)*

21. In which book do you read about the death of Moses? *(Deuteronomy)*

22. Name the two books of the Bible that have women's names. *(Ruth, Esther)*

23. In which book do we read about Joseph? *(Genesis)*

24. In which book do we read about the conversion of Saul (Paul)? *(Acts)*

25. In which book and chapter do we first read about Abraham? *(Genesis 11)*

26. In which book do we find the Ten commandments first given? *(Exodus)*

27. In which book do we read about the three men thrown into the fiery furnace? *(Daniel)*

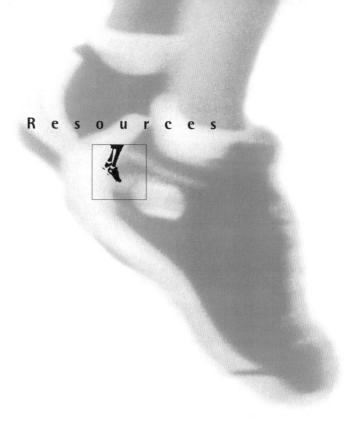

R e s o u r c e s

Memory Verses

Over 100 Memory Verses from the New Testament!

Matthew

5:13	You are the salt ...
5:14	You are the light ...
6:33	Seek first the kingdom of God ...
9:37	Then he said to his disciples ...
11:28	Come to me, all you who are weary ...
13:49	This is how it will be at the end of the age ...
24:42	Therefore keep watch ...
28:19	Therefore go and make disciples of ...

Mark

1:15	'The time has come ...
8:34(b)	'If anyone would come after me ... (and 35–38!)
10:45	... the Son of Man did not come to be served, but to serve ...

Luke

1:68	'Praise be to the Lord ...
2:10	But the angel said to them ...
5:31,32	Jesus answered them, 'It is not the healthy who need ...
6:27	But I tell you ... (love your enemies)
6:31	Do to others as you would have ...
9:23	... take up his cross daily ...
12:15	'Watch out! Be on your guard against ...

John

1:1-2	In the beginning ...
1:18	No-one has ever seen God ...
3:16	For God so loved the world ...
6:28-29	... 'The work of God is to believe in the one he sent.'
6:44	'No-one can come to the father unless the father draws him ...
8:31-32	... the truth shall set you free.
10:10	... they may have life, and life to the full.
11:25	I am the resurrection and the life ...
13:24-35	A new command ... love one another ...
14:6	I am the way and the ...
14:15	if you love me ...
20:30-31	Jesus did many other ... but these are written so ...

Acts

2:42	They devoted themselves ... to prayer.
4:12	salvation is found in no-one else ...

Romans

1:16	I am not ashamed ...
3:23-24	for all have sinned and fall short ...
5:8	But God demonstrates his own love for us in this ...
8:28	In all things God works for the good of ...
10:9	If you confess with your mouth ...
12:1-2	Do not conform ...
12:18	if it is possible, as for as it depends on you, live at peace ...

1 Corinthians

1:27	... God chose the weak things of the world ...
10:12-13	if you think you are standing firm ... tempted he will also provide a way out
15:3-4	... Christ died ... our sins according to the Scriptures ...
15:58	... stand firm. Let nothing move you ...

2 Corinthians

4:2	... we have renounced secret and shameful ...

4:18	so we fix our eyes not on what is seen ...
5:17	Therefore, if anyone is in Christ he is a new creation ...
5:21	God made him who had no sin ...
10:4	The weapons we fight with are not the ...
11:14	... for Satan masquerades as an angel of light.

Galatians
1:8	But even if we or an angel ...
2:20	I have been crucified with Christ ...
3:13	Christ redeemed us from the curse
3:28	... neither Jew nor Greek ...
5:22-23	But the fruit of the Spirit is ...
6:2	Carry each other's burdens

Ephesians
1:4	For he chose us in him before the creation of the world
1:13	Having believed, you were marked ...
2:8-9	For it is by grace you have been saved ...
4:26-27	In your anger do not sin ...
4:29	Do not let any unwholesome talk ...
6:13	Therefore put on the full armour of God ...

Philippians
1:6	... he who began a good work in you ...
1:21	For to me, to live is Christ ...
2:1-11	... Your attitude should be the same as that of Christ Jesus ...
3:13-14	... I press on towards the goal to win the prize ...
4:4-7	Rejoice in the Lord always ...

Colossians
1:21-22	Once you were alienated ...
1:28-29	We proclaim him, admonishing ....
3:16	Let the word of Christ dwell in you richly as you teach ...
3:17	And whatever you do whether in word or speech ...
3:23	Whatever you do, work at it with all your heart ...
4:2	Devote yourselves to prayer ...
4:5-6	Be wise in the way you act towards outsiders ...

1 Thessalonians
2:13	And we also thank God continually because ...
3:12	May the Lord make your love increase ...
4:11,12	Make it your ambition to lead a quiet life ...
4:14	We believe that Jesus died and rose again ...
5:4,5	But you, brothers, are not in darkness ...

5:16–18   Be joyful always; ...

2 Thessalonians
1:8   He will punish those who do not know God ...
3:10   For even when we were with you ...

1 Timothy
4:8   For physical training is of some value ...
4:12   Don't let anyone look down on you because you are young ...
4:16   Watch your life and doctrine closely
6:6   But godliness with contentment ...

2 Timothy
3:12   ... everyone who wants to live a godly life in Christ ...
3:16   All scripture is God-breathed ...
4:2   Preach the word. Be prepared ...
4:7   I have fought the good fight ...

Titus
2:11–12   For the grace of God that brings salvation has appeared to all men ...
3:4–5   But when the kindness and love of God our Saviour appeared ...

Hebrews
1:1–2   In the past God spoke to our forefathers ...
4:12   For the word of God is living and active ...
4:15   Tempted in every way, just as we are ...
9:27   Just as man is destined to die once
10:25   Let us not give up meeting together ...
11:1   Now faith is ...
12:1-3   Therefore, since we are surrounded by such a great cloud of witnesses ...
13:8   Jesus Christ is the same yesterday and today and forever

James
1:5   If any of you lacks wisdom ...
1:22   Do not merely listen to the word ...
2:19   You believe that there is one God. Good! ...
4:7   Resist the devil and he will flee

1 Peter
1:18   It was not with perishable things such as silver or gold
2:9   But you are a chosen people ...
2:24   He himself bore our sins in his body ...
3:15   But in your hearts set apart Christ as Lord
3:18   For Christ died for sins once for all ...
5:7   Cast all your anxiety on him ...

2 Peter

1:16	We did not follow cleverly invented stories ...
1:21	For prophecy never had its origin ...
3:8	But do not forget this one thing ...

1 John

1:8-9	If we claim to be without sin ...
3:1	How great is the love of the Father ...
3:16	This is how we know what love is ...
4:10	This is love: not that we loved God, but ...
5:11-12	He who has the Son has life ...
5:13 I	write these things ...

2 John

| 4 | It has given me great joy to find ... |
| 7 | Many deceivers who do not acknowledge Jesus ... |

3 John

| 2 | Dear friend, I pray that you may enjoy ... |
| 11 | Dear friend, do not imitate what is evil but ... |

Jude

20	But you, dear friends, build yourselves up in ...
21	Keep yourselves in God's love as ...
22,23	Be merciful to those who doubt ...
24,25	To him who is able to keep you...

Revelation

1:8	I am the Alpha and the ...
1:18	I am the Living One: I was dead ...
3:20	Here I am! I stand at the door ...
4:11	You are worthy, our Lord and God ...
5:12	In a loud voice they sang: 'Worthy ...
7:9	After this I looked and there before me was a great ...
7:17	For the Lamb at the centre of the throne will be ...
11:15(b)	'The kingdom of the world has become the ...
12:11	They overcame him by the blood of the Lamb ...
15:3(b)	'Great and marvellous are your deeds ...
16:15	'Behold, I come like a thief! Blessed ...
20:15	If anyone's name was not found ...
21:4	He will wipe every tear from their ...
22:17	The Spirit and the bride say ...

Predicament verses

Here are some Predicaments we have done together with the Bible verses we printed and handed out to the group.

1. You are tempted to go out with someone who is not a follower of Jesus

For the nation of Israel, it was forbidden to marry outside the faith. Malachi 2:11–12

2 Kings 11:1-13 Learn from King Solomon's mistake!

The message of the New Testament is to be wise, careful, and always put Jesus first. You must also realise that you are very different!

1 Corinthians 7:39,40 ... a widow must marry a Christian

2 Corinthians 6:14 ... be careful of who you are 'tied' to!

1 Corinthians 7 ... it is quite ok to stay single!

1 Corinthians 10:12 ... 'take care so that you don't fall!'

Colossians 1:21,22 ... 'Once you were separate from God ... but now ...'

1 Peter 2:9,10 ... But you are a chosen people, a royal priesthood, a holy nation, a people belonging to God, that you may declare the praises of him who called you out of darkness into his wonderful light. [10] Once you were not a people, but now you are the people of God; once you had not received mercy, but now you have received mercy.

2. You have a fight with friends. Or, you get angry with your church (and want to leave)

Galatians 5:22 ... But the fruit of the Spirit is love, joy, peace, patience, kindness, goodness, faithfulness, gentleness and self-control.

2 Peter 1:5-7 ... For this very reason, make every effort to add to your faith goodness; and to goodness, knowledge; and to knowledge, self-control; and to self-control, perseverance; and to perseverance, godliness; and to godliness, brotherly kindness; and to brotherly kindness, love.

The core message of the Bible is love, reconciliation & forgiveness. Be clear on this.

God reconciled us to himself:

2 Corinthians 5:18 ... All this is from God, who reconciled us to himself through Christ ...

Colossians 1:22 ... But now he has reconciled you by Christ's physical body through death to present you holy in his sight, without blemish and free from accusation

God forgave us, therefore we must forgive others:

Ephesians 4:32 ... Be kind and compassionate to one another, forgiving each other, just as in Christ God forgave you.

Colossians 3:13 ... Bear with each other and forgive whatever grievances you may have against one another. Forgive as the Lord forgave you.

How we must treat others (and those in our church):

Matthew 5:23–24 ... 'Therefore, if you are offering your gift at the altar and there remember that your brother has something against you, leave your gift there in front of the altar. First go and be reconciled to your brother; then come and offer your gift.'

Luke 12:58 ... As you are going with your adversary to the magistrate, try hard to be reconciled to him on the way, or he may drag you off to the judge, and the judge turn you over to the officer, and the officer throw you into prison.

1 Peter 3:8,9 ... Finally, all of you, live in harmony with one another; be sympathetic, love as brothers, be compassionate and humble. Do not repay evil with evil or insult with insult, but with blessing, because to this you were called so that you may inherit a blessing.

Matthew 18:15–17 ... If your brother sins against you ...

3. You have to forgive someone for a wrong they have done to you.

Luke 17:3 ... So watch yourselves. "'If your brother sins, rebuke him, and if he repents, forgive him. ⁴ If he sins against you seven times in a day, and seven times comes back to you and says, 'I repent,' forgive him."

2 Corinthians 2:7 ... Now instead, you ought to forgive and comfort him, so that he will not be overwhelmed by excessive sorrow.

2 Corinthians 2:10 ... If you forgive anyone, I also forgive him. And what I have forgiven – if there was anything to forgive – I have forgiven in the sight of Christ for your sake,

Colossians 3:13 ... Bear with each other and forgive whatever grievances you may have against one another. Forgive as the Lord forgave you.

4. You are tempted to make excuses (and perhaps lie)

Proverbs 12:17 ... A truthful witness gives honest testimony, but a false witness tells lies.

Proverbs 24:26 ... An honest answer is like a kiss on the lips.

Proverbs 12:19 ... Truthful lips endure forever, but a lying tongue lasts only a moment.

Proverbs. 12:22 ... The LORD detests lying lips, but he delights in men who are truthful.

Proverbs 14:5 ... A truthful witness does not deceive, but a false witness pours out lies.

Proverb. 14:25 ... A truthful witness saves lives, but a false witness is deceitful.

Proverbs 16:11 ... Honest scales and balances are from the LORD; all the weights in the bag are of his making.

Proverbs 16:13 ... Kings take pleasure in honest lips; they value a man who speaks the truth.

Proverbs 25:13 ... Like the coolness of snow at harvest time is a trustworthy messenger to those who send him; he refreshes the spirit of his masters.

Matthew 5:37 Simply let your 'Yes' be 'Yes,' and your 'No,' 'No'; anything beyond this comes from the evil one.

Luke 14:16–25 Jesus replied: "A certain man was preparing a great banquet and invited many guests. At the time of the banquet he sent his servant to tell those who had been invited, 'Come, for everything is now ready.'" But they all alike began to make excuses ...

Colossians. 3:9 Do not lie to each other, since you have taken off your old self with its practices

James 5:12 ... Above all, my brothers, do not swear – not by heaven or by earth or by anything else. Let your 'Yes' be yes, and your 'No,' no, or you will be condemned.

5. What do you if you are hassled by a beggar on a train (or the street)?

Proverbs 3:27 ... Do not withhold good from those who deserve it, when it is in your power to act.

However, Proverbs 19:24 ... The sluggard buries his hand in the dish; he will not even bring it back to his mouth!

Luke 6:31 ... Do to others as you would have them do to you.

Galatians 6:10 ... Therefore, as we have opportunity, let us do good to all people, especially to those who belong to the family of believers.

2 Thessalonians 3:10 ... For even when we were with you, we gave you this rule: 'If a man will not work, he shall not eat.'

6. Someone puts pressure on you to do things sexually?

1 Corinthians 6:18 ... Flee from sexual immorality. All other sins a man commits are outside his body, but he who sins sexually sins against his own body.

1 Corinthians 10:12,13 ... So, if you think you are standing firm, be careful that you don't fall! No temptation has seized you except what is common to man. And God is faithful; he will not let you be tempted beyond what you can bear. But when you are tempted, he will also provide a way out so that you can stand up under it.

1 Thessalonians 4:3-7 ... It is God's will that you should be sanctified: that you should avoid sexual immorality; that each of you should learn to control his own body in a way that is holy and honourable, not in passionate lust like the heathen, who do not know God; and that in this matter no one should wrong his brother or take advantage of him. The Lord will punish men for all such sins, as we have already told you and warned you. For God did not call us to be impure, but to live a holy life.

1 Timothy 5:1 ... Do not rebuke an older man harshly, but exhort him as if he were your father. Treat younger men as brothers, older women as mothers, and younger women as sisters, with absolute purity.

Titus 2:11,12 ... For the grace of God that brings salvation has appeared to all men. It teaches us to say 'No' to ungodliness and worldly passions, and to live self-controlled, upright and godly lives in this present age.

7. Someone puts pressure on you to drink alcohol?

Proverbs 20:1 ... Wine is a mocker and beer a brawler; whoever is led astray by them is not wise.

1 Corinthians 6:10 ... nor thieves nor the greedy nor drunkards nor slanderers nor swindlers will inherit the kingdom of God.

Galatians 5:19-21 ... The acts of the sinful nature are obvious: sexual immorality, impurity and debauchery; idolatry and witchcraft; hatred, discord, jealousy, fits of rage, selfish ambition, dissensions, factions and envy; drunkenness, orgies, and the like. I warn you, as I did before, that those who live like this will not inherit the kingdom of God.

Ephesians 5:18 ... Do not get drunk on wine, which leads to debauchery. Instead, be filled with the Spirit.

Titus 1:7 ... Since an overseer is entrusted with God's work, he must be blameless – not overbearing, not quick-tempered, not given to drunkenness.